The Soviet Syndrome

The Soviet

Foreword by Raymond Aron | Translated by Patricia Ran

Syndrome

Alain Besançon

Harcourt Brace Jovanovich | **New York and London**

Printed in the United States of America

Library of Congress Cataloging in Publication Data

Besançon, Alain.
   The Soviet syndrome.

   Translation of Court traité de soviétologie.
   1. Communism—Russia—History. I. Title.
HX313.B4513   335.43′0947   77–26979
ISBN 0–15–184603–0

First edition

B C D E

For my friends Emilio, Paz, and Juan Miguel

Any sound thinking in the analysis you are about to read is the product of a circle of friends. I am aware of my great indebtedness to countless conversations with Kostas Papaioannou and Annie Kriegel. The reading public will find in Annie Kriegel's extensive works a number of the points arranged here in a different sequence. Raymond Aron showed me what political reasoning is. I am solely responsible for the theses contained in this brief treatise.

Alain Besançon

Contents

Foreword

The Soviet Syndrome by my friend Alain Besançon may surprise the reader. I do not want to spoil the pleasant surprise in store for him. Rather than risk writing a postscript instead of a foreword, I shall not discuss this thought-provoking, aggressive text, written in one spurt and animated by a sort of intellectual lightness, as if to stress the contrast between the interpreter and the subject being studied.

Since Stalin's death, the majority of Westerners have become convinced that the Soviet Union is a country "like any other," that the regime is comparable to the regimes encountered over the centuries—despotic, it is true, tolerating no opposition, and with no free elections, but in line with the old despotisms of Asia and even Europe. The most optimistic observers predicted convergence: why wouldn't a capitalism undergoing socialization and a socialism undergoing liberalization move closer together on the historical horizon, until they seemed mere variations of the same sort of society? After all, on both sides the forces or means of production are yielding ground to the same rationality. One does not have to be a Marxist to agree that machines shape those who use them, and organizations, those who serve them.

Another form of layman's Marxism was prone to an even more optimistic vision: if the Soviets lowered the Iron Curtain in order to hide the cruelties of primitive accumulation, why shouldn't they lift it once they had caught up with, if not surpassed, capitalism? They would restore freedom—or at least certain freedoms—to the individual the moment that, as Khrushchev said, they could butter their spinach and offer everyone a good goulash. This would-be wisdom, typical of those who pride themselves on being clairvoyant because they are free from common passions, is being rudely shaken by such Russian dissidents as Andrei Sakharov and Alexander Solzhenitsyn.

Here is a superpower that possesses some fifty percent more intercontinental ballistic missiles than the United States. The minimum monthly wage totals sixty rubles, the average wage one hundred and ten (officially, one hundred and thirty). According to Sakharov, the buying power of the minimum wage is roughly thirty dollars. Even if you double that estimate, even if you take into account free or inexpensive social services, the standard of living is incredibly low compared with that of Western Europe (Spain included). A family of four with a three-room apartment is among the privileged, and in most cases a protégé of someone in power.

Here is a regime that offers itself as a model, that claims to show the way to salvation for all mankind: a half century after the Revolution of 1917, it is buying tens of millions of tons of grain abroad, and forbidding ordinary citizens to leave the homeland of socialism. Along the frontiers of the People's Democratic Republic—in the no man's land between the two worlds—attack dogs continually patrol, sniffing out any traitors who might be choosing liberty. Between the two Germanies, the Berlin Wall symbolizes the meaning that the men in the Kremlin and in Pankow give to "peaceful coexistence": they are in possession of the truth, but refuse all dialogue.

What unusual characteristic sets the Soviet Union apart from the classic despotism or tyranny? What explains the faithfulness of true believers and their fear of infidels—an often indelible mark that Marxism-Leninism leaves upon those who have sworn fidelity and then recant? One word supplies both the answer and the basic premise of this analysis: *ideology*. Westerners wanted to forget about ideology; first Solzhenitsyn, then Besançon in his *Soviet Syndrome,* remind us—each in his own way—that we can understand nothing about Lenin or Stalin or even Brezhnev, if we overlook the doctrine (or the dogma or faith—the exact word is unimportant) in the name of which a Marxist sect seized power and undertook the reconstruction of the world or the construction of socialism.

The Bolsheviks had retained a crude version of Marx's prophecy: a radical break between capitalism and socialism; the impossibility of any compromise between the two, or even of reaching a compromise through reform; hence the expectation of, and the desire for, a revolution transfigured into a sort of advent of truth; a final condemnation of private property (in its broadest sense) and of the market, two institutions that are once and for all excommunicated as inseparable from the capitalist sin. An intransigent and quarrelsome sect within Russian social democracy (which was itself one of the weak links in the chain of the Second International)—a sect accustomed and forced to be clandestine—the Bolsheviks, and, even more, Lenin himself, believed themselves vested with the historical mission that Marx had entrusted to the proletariat, and that the Second International had entrusted to social democracy. As the only authentic representative of social democracy—which itself represented the proletariat—they drew no distinction between their power and the power of the working class (or of the worker-peasant coalition). Sixty years after the days that shook the world, they still think as they did in exile or as émigrés. Lenin's fanaticism was transformed into the orthodoxy of an empire.

Despite disagreements that are more apparent than real (or in any event minor), the physicist and the novelist who came out of the cold concur with one another, and with the French Sovietologist, about the basis of any understanding of the *Soviet specimen:* the regime was built by true believers who collided, and are still colliding, with the insurmountable resistance of things—that is, the nature of man and society. The socialism of which they dreamed does not, and in the foreseeable future never will, exist. Yet for the moment at least, the Bolsheviks will not give up their ideology: despite Solzhenitsyn's pleas, they will not confess to their illusions and their errors, even if Solzhenitsyn is correct in writing: "For a long time now, everything has rested solely on material calculation and the subjection of the people, and not on any upsurge of ideological enthusiasm."*

Throughout history, regimes or (if you prefer) the ruling class—sovereigns and privileged persons—have tended to justify themselves by invoking a legitimizing principle. Obviously, Marxism-Leninism is the legitimizing principle of the Soviet regime. It transfigures the reign of the Party, or

* Alexander Solzhenitsyn, *Letter to the Soviet Leaders,* trans. Hilary Sternberg (New York: Harper & Row, 1974), p. 46.

of an oligarchy within the Party, or of a man within the oligarchy, into a step toward human salvation. If the Party ceased viewing itself as the vanguard of the proletariat, it would become the collective tyrant, the Prince who governs according to his mood and his own personal advantage. But the Party does not wish to be a tyrant; if it retains exclusive power, it is because such power is inseparable from the proletariat and socialism. Those Party members who, in their hearts, view the Party (or the oligarchy that rules it) as a tyrant, are guilty of the deviation that Besançon calls cynicism: a rightist deviation that draws no distinction between Machiavellian methods, which are inevitable during any war, and Machiavellian philosophy.

In order to avoid this rightist deviation, it is not enough that the Party be entrusted with the revolutionary task; the Party, which holds the reins of power, has to build socialism. What does socialism consist of? Lenin probably would have given a different answer from Brezhnev, and perhaps the latter would give no answer at all. On the other hand, both agree on the same refusals: the refusal to permit private ownership of the instruments of production, and the refusal to permit the "market form" —in other words, commercial exchanges and, if need be, money. The Bolsheviks knew nothing about managing a modern economy, for Marxism had imposed a major excommunication upon these methods of organization. Hence the collision between the Party (or the partisan State) and civil society, and hence too the alternation between periods of tension and periods of relaxation, as described by Besançon. At times the Party or the State makes maximum use of the means of constraint to force civil society to comply with the law of the ideology, whereas at other times it allows the peasants in the kolkhozy to cultivate their plots of ground, or allows Solzhenitsyn to publish *One Day in the Life of Ivan Denisovich.*

As 1976 dawned, the leaders and peoples of the states of Eastern Europe seemed to fear a new period of tension, a renewed struggle against "capitalist survivals" and against a massive counterattack by the "classes condemned by history." Such a period would be profoundly different from "War Communism," as Lenin and his companions tried to conduct it. No one in the Kremlin considers sending soldiers to wrest wheat from the peasants, or getting along without money. Administrators accept the "market form," even when manifested as the black market. In other words, the cycles of tension and détente involve an orientation: the Bolsheviks remain ideologists, but have resigned themselves to compromise with a rebellious reality. Nicolas S. Timasheff, the sociologist who named his book on the Soviet Union of the 1930s *The Great Retreat,* began to gloat too quickly, and did not notice the offensive that had preceded each of the retreats. Each failure of the offensive had nonetheless left imprints upon the leaders' minds. Today none of them would write *The State and the Revolution* as Lenin had done.

Of course the lesson learned from War Communism did not offer protection from the excesses of agrarian collectivization. Shortly after seizing power, while a climate of civil war still prevailed, the Bolsheviks tried to impose a distribution of property by reducing trade to a minimum. Eight years after the first retreat, Stalin probably thought he would decrease the kulaks' consumption, and increase the total amount appropriated from the harvest to aid the cities, if in rural areas he eliminated the distinction between rich and poor, between those who possessed something and those who owned nothing. At that time he even launched a war between the State and the peasantry; the latter was defeated, although the victor did not attain his economic or political objectives.

Each phase, called "War Communism" or "NEP" ("New Economic Policy") has its special characteristics. In the economy, from the first phase, which is symbolized by the substitution of bayonets for money, to the third phase, which followed the victory of 1945—a phase symbolized by the rebuilding of the kolkhozy and the continued subordination of consumer goods to investment—the historian tends to discern a drawing together of ideology and reality, a training period for economic mechanisms which, it is true, are still paralyzed by psychological blocks not yet overcome in our day. The men in the Kremlin know the means available to improve agricultural production; but they continue to prefer the logic of their ideology to the logic of productivity —showing what Westerners mistakenly call "irrationality," as if deeds ever followed a single line of logic.

The Soviet Union will not repeat War Communism and agrarian collectivization in any form, any more than it will re-enact in the future the Great Purge and the ceremonial trial confessions. The reign of terror and the concentration camp were born in the days of Lenin's rise to power. The verbal violence with which the militant Lenin, head of the Bolshevik faction, accused of treason those comrades who did not agree with his interpretation of an article of the dogma was transmuted into actual violence. The Bolshevik faction, which claimed to represent the worker-peasant coalition, was nonetheless a sect that faced the hostility of the bulk of the population. It never left off excluding traitors and hounding enemies. While he played the role of Zurich-based interpreter of historical truth, Lenin used irony;

when he acted as bearer of both the sword of might and the scales of justice, he inspired terror. Yet let us not rob Stalin of his own personal possession: the destruction of the Leninist Party in order to create another—truly Stalinist—Party.

Is the past permanently past? Let us not forget that the current liberalization has its limits. There are still from one to one and a half million people in concentration camps, and from five to ten thousand dissidents confined to insane asylums. Compared with the other phases—the phase of the Great Purge and that of the last years of Stalin—the current period is one of détente (although it involves certain signs of tension compared to the good old days of Khrushchev). This does not mean that the Bolsheviks have made peace with society and human nature. Tomorrow they may launch an attack against the improvised citadels where workers and intellectuals, peasants and artisans seek refuge, when the winds of the ideological and terrorist storm start to blow. Yet in spite of everything, in this oligarchy of old men I find it hard to imagine some exceptional individual appearing—a cynic or a naive man whom hatred or ambition would drive to exploits like Lenin's or Stalin's. And politically the new offensive, should it begin, would seem like a retreat, when compared with earlier periods of terrorism.

Whether ideocratic or logocratic, the Soviet regime shares one trait with the despotisms of the past: its apparent immutability. Time does not advance at the same rate there as in the democratic societies, whose permanent agitation creates the impression—not always correct—of rapid change. The constancy of Sovietism, the unrelenting attempt to make civil society subject to the law of the Party, the leaders' refusal to see themselves and their work as they really are—an empire-building despotism, and not a social-ism bringing personal freedom—all this prevents Western-ers from thinking that they are face to face with a regime "like any other." They are confronted by the Union of Soviet Socialist Republics—and not, as De Gaulle pretended to believe, by Russia. A sect which claims (and believes) that it is constructing socialism has glued a sizable system of production and first-rate military equipment, like a veneer, upon a country that in many respects is still primi-tive. Only ideology bridges the gap between the prosaic reality and the millennial interpretation of it.

In a frequently quoted passage of his letter to Soviet leaders, Solzhenitsyn writes: "This universal, obligatory force-feeding with lies is now the most agonizing aspect of existence in our country—worse than all our material miseries, worse than any lack of civil liberties."*

Perhaps, at the risk of being pedantic, I should expand upon Besançon and sketch out a typology of *lies*. In the exact, strict sense of the word, he who consciously says the opposite of the truth is lying: Lenin's companions were lying when they confessed to crimes they had not commit-ted, and Soviet propaganda was lying when it sang of the happiness of the people during the days of agrarian col-lectivization; Trotsky was not a Gestapo agent, and Tuka-chevsky was not one either.

On the other hand, when the Bolsheviks, the Communists, call the Soviet Union *socialist*, must we say that they are lying? Everything depends upon one's definition of social-ism. If socialism implies individual freedom or equal pay, of course the Bolsheviks and the Communists are lying. But if they recognize the distance between what socialism is today and what it will be when it conforms to its essence,

* Solzhenitsyn, *Letter,* p. 47.

then they are not, in the strictest sense, lying, but, rather, substituting for reality what Besançon calls "pseudo reality": the meaning that they give something in terms of a future they imagine as conforming to the ideology. Despite everything, Sovietism signifies a step along the road to socialism, and hence a step toward the salvation of all mankind.

How does one refute this interpretation, in the sense of bringing to an end its significance? One must make a plausible, if not scientific, judgment about the link between collective ownership and government planning on the one hand, and the human values of socialism on the other. In the intellectual circles of the West, criticism of capitalism has spread the presumption that collective ownership and government planning as such possess moral virtues, because private ownership and the market partake of the capitalist sin. But historical experience indicates an incompatibility, rather than an obligatory link, between economic modalities and socialist ideals. Unfortunately, only the skeptic or the rationalist prefers experience to faith.

I am reminded of a remark by Guy Mollet, Premier of the Fourth Republic, who in a meeting shouted out: "They tell us our policy has failed—is that any reason for giving it up?" For over half a century the Bolsheviks have been using this maxim to their advantage. Mollet's remark brought laughter; Stalin did not make people laugh, nor did Khrushchev, nor does Brezhnev. Compared with the goals of their ideology, the Bolsheviks' policy has failed. Does the number of divisions and intercontinental ballistic missiles compensate for that failure? In any event, this is no laughing matter.

Raymond Aron

The Two Faces of the System

An up-to-date comprehension of the U.S.S.R. requires continual effort. Not because fundamental changes are occurring within the regime: quite the contrary, its extraordinary stasis is one of the reasons why we find it hard to keep our comprehension up to date, since we expect a regime, a country, sooner or later to follow the historical rhythm of other countries. The chief problem confronting the expert in Soviet affairs is not to keep his information up to date, as it is in other fields. His main difficulty lies in accepting as true what most people deem improbable, in believing the unbelievable. Twenty years ago very few experts in Soviet affairs accepted at face value the obviously absurd figures provided by objective data. It would have seemed insane to propose the figure of sixty million dead, as Alexander Solzhenitsyn is now doing, without causing much of a stir. (According to Kurganov about thirty million were killed during the war, and another thirty million either were executed, died of starvation during collectivization, or did not survive deportation.) Today we are tempted to shrug our shoulders at Andrei Sakharov's estimate that in 1975 the average monthly salary in the U.S.S.R. was fifty-five dollars, while the minimum salary was thirty dollars.

Above all, our main difficulty consists in remaining

mentally within a universe whose co-ordinates bear no relationship to our own. This sensation of passing through the looking glass is disagreeable and psychologically difficult to tolerate for very long. And so the general picture, rather than the individual details, becomes blurred. If we take the trouble, we can manage to comprehend the whole of the U.S.S.R. and communism. If we relax our efforts, our comprehension will falter as a whole. Perhaps this is what happened during the past decade to those countries that set out to understand the U.S.S.R. and succeeded. Their experts wearied of focusing continually upon such an unattractive and static object. They turned their eyes upon more cheerful and varied regions. At that point public opinion, left with no counterbalance, chimed in with the press, and leaders allowed themselves to be influenced by public opinion. And so, over the years, a very loosely woven body of opinions triumphed, and no crises occurred to make us question them. In this field, only urgency and imminent danger call for concerted attention.

For the past few years we have been resting our heads on the soft cushion of "détente," and no urgent issues involving us have forced us to refine our concepts. We do not want to be bothered by the voices of Soviet dissidents, loud though they be. Despite their commercial success, books by dissidents—even those by Solzhenitsyn—have not, it seems, affected the gamut of public opinion or the serenity of our leaders. So in the end we are lulled by imprecise analyses, and settle for demonstrating our prudence about overly restrictive commitments, and our "realism" (as we call it) about the tangible advantages of East-West trade.

But it seems that more recently—at least since early 1975—our rest is becoming less peaceful than we hoped.

4

In addition to the dissidents, the Chinese government has been warning us for a long time about the illusions of détente. The Chinese are losing no opportunity to warn Europeans of the military danger that, according to them, weighs upon Europe even more than China. They are urging us to speed up the political and especially the military unification of Europe. They are playing the role of last believers in the Atlantic Alliance, of latter-day disciples of John Foster Dulles. Nor can we, despite soothing words from the Soviet government, close our eyes to various acts of subversion and espionage, or believe that the Soviets are totally innocent as regards the disasters in South Vietnam, the tensions in the Middle East, or even the Yom Kippur War, or attempts to assume power in Portugal. There has been reason to wonder whether "détente" is not purely and simply a hypocrisy, a deceitful cloud that in actual fact covers up an aggressive policy, just as the Chinese and the Soviet dissidents have been saying time and again. But even this is not clear.

Indeed, instead of persevering in their apparently very profitable duplicity, since the summer of 1975 Soviet leaders have been openly trying a bit of calculated insolence, have dished out a few rebuffs, and have allowed some "hard-line," "ideological," and "revolutionary" articles to appear in *Pravda*. They no longer shake hands, no longer "joke with photographers," no longer smile for television, appear severe, cold, grouchy. And we are asking ourselves: Do they want to go back to the Cold War? Should we put Brezhnev among the doves? Shouldn't we support the "soft-liners" against the "hard-liners," the "pragmatists" against the "dogmatists"? Wouldn't it be appropriate to lure them with economic advantages, to tie them in a lasting way to the West, to send them massive shipments of grain, and even

5

technology since they are requesting it? Indeed, the Soviets are asking for wheat and technology, and also, in order to buy them, long-term loans at preferential rates. But at the same time they talk of class struggle, dictatorship of the proletariat, and ideological vigilance. So just what is going on? How is it possible to accumulate a debt that ran in excess of seventeen billion dollars in 1975 and forty-five billion by early 1977, and at the same time dig the grave of the monopolistic capitalism of the State? If it were really the aim of Soviet leaders to expropriate the possessions of the lenders in a Machiavellian way, would they talk publicly about expropriation?

No over-all view of Soviet communism can be conveyed in these few pages. But it is possible to construct a schema of Soviet foreign policy that will not contradict what we know about communism. I will discuss only one general theme: the relationship between the current imperatives of Soviet domestic and foreign policy.

There are two, and only two, general models of Soviet policy. Since they were put into practice during the very first years of the regime, I shall use their original names: *War Communism* and *NEP,* or New Economic Policy. By "War Communism" I mean the Communist Party's efforts to force civil society to become a part of the plan predetermined by the ideology. In 1917 the Communist Party had a clear vision of the form that society spontaneously would assume, once "bourgeois" power was overthrown and "proletarian" power, as represented by the Bolshevik Party, was established. Things did not go as expected. Social groups, individuals, and economic developments followed a course that was entirely different from the one predicted. War Communism, therefore, was a violent effort to force

things and men into the sphere in which the Party thought
and acted.

By "NEP" I mean a certain relaxation of ideological
power, and a certain latitude given to civil society to organize as it saw fit. The NEP was born of the failure of War
Communism. Those in power had come to realize that, as
they gradually extended their violent control over civil
society, the latter was being killed, while the new institutions projected for civil society remained stillborn.
If they persisted in this direction, power itself risked col-
lapsing because, as it extended its coercive force to the
totality of men and things, the wellsprings of that force ran
dry.

From this perspective, the relationship between power
and civil society might be compared to that between a
parasite and its host. If the host begins to weaken, the parasite sooner or later meets the same fate. Sometimes a rather
stable symbiosis develops between the parasite, which gives
up trying to invade the entire organism, and the host, which
for its part cannot become altogether healthy. During the
past sixty years—ever since the October Revolution—there
has been no evidence of such an equilibrium. Instead, there
have been very pronounced oscillations; by the end of each
swing, civil society has all but been annihilated, or power
all but been eliminated or assimilated.

I am not disregarding the drawbacks in naming two
political models, or two ideal types, after two unique and
unreproducible historical situations. But in the Soviet vocabulary—which I intend to follow closely—these names
also designate two political *lines* of the Party which have
been employed since the very first years of the regime, and
which I believe will be revived in future contexts. These
models do not exist in their pure state: they are analytical

tools for interpreting concrete situations. I shall henceforth use "War Communism" and "NEP," and later "détente" and "Cold War," in their customary and abstract sense.

The first War Communism lasted from 1917 to 1921. Its assault upon all classes was so brutal, so total, that society was almost destroyed by famine, sickness, shock.

In 1921, rejecting the advice of Trotsky and the "radicals," who would have preferred continuing the experiment at the risk of losing power, the Bolshevik Party decided to beat a tactical retreat. At that time it controlled the State, the cities, the working class, and the intelligentsia. It temporarily relinquished its hold over the peasantry. The greater part of the population, the peasant world, was thus in a sense penned up within limits assigned to it, but inside which it enjoyed a certain autonomy. The peasant could plant, sow, harvest, and sell as he wished. He was thus in a position to keep the country alive and consequently provide support for Soviet power, which had by no means abandoned its utopian ambitions, even though it had pulled in its horns quite a way. It used this period of respite to consolidate its advances, build up an executive staff, continue the ideological education of its members, strengthen discipline within the Party, and gain more complete control over the social groups under its direct authority.

However, the existence of an autonomous sphere was dangerous in the long run. It was per se contrary to doctrinal predictions and brought a destructive incoherence into the ideology. Keeping to biological metaphors, we might say that ideological power cannot be compared with a trichina, which is content to feed upon surrounding tissues without transforming them. It more closely resembles the cancerous cells that transfer their own growth code to normal cells, which in turn become malignant, so that the cancer strives to transform the entire organism into a widespread cancer, patterned after the original cancerous cell. If it does not succeed, it may shrink and gradually be eliminated by the buildup of young, healthy cells.

This comparison is possible to the degree that the ideology incorporates a plan for reorganizing the world, a plan born of an omniscience that has grasped the fundamental laws of that world and can predict its evolution. The Party is the alliance among men who are possessed of the ideology, and who therefore think in terms of the new reality it promises. If the old reality persists unchanged within the circle of power, its very existence contradicts the reality of ideological pseudo reality and constantly threatens to destroy it. In both the social and political spheres, the reconstitution of civil society—that is, the organization of groups where once there had been merely a welter of social atoms powerless before the single Party—impairs Party unity. Social pluralism may be reflected in the Party itself, which soon will be divided into factions, and will watch out more or less for the specific social concerns of one or another segment of the population.

That is why, in the late 1920s, the Party decided to resume its offensive against the peasantry and thus gain control of the entire population. Politically, it was up to the task. Hence the Party was able, without serious political harm, to go through the horrendous crisis of collectivization, which brought in its wake a murderous famine, the permanent destruction of Soviet agriculture, and the installation of a lasting reign of terror. Collectivization was a national but not a political catastrophe; or, if you prefer, it was a disaster for reality but not for pseudo reality.

And so War Communism II began. Stalin was intentionally inspired by the methods used in the first one. Yet this new War Communism was no more successful at building viable institutions than its predecessor. There were no kolkhozy (in the sense of co-operative farms), only slave plantations; no government economic planning (save in the imagination of Western economists), only a wartime economy capable of concentrating its efforts on arsenals, while leaving the rest in disorder; no economy in the strict sense of the word, since no self-regulating system developed, and since econometric calculations were impossible where all bookkeeping was impossible.

The U.S.S.R. therefore entered World War II in a very perilous situation. Tens of millions of people either had starved to death during collectivization, had been killed during political purges, or were still locked up in concentration camps. The military staff had been decimated. There had been an almost total turnover in the Party itself, for Stalin wanted to set up a new Party entirely of his own creation. He therefore exterminated the old Party, even though almost all its members had been devoted to him. Initial defeats made the adoption of a new NEP an urgent matter.

NEP II differed noticeably from its predecessor. Not that there was a relaxation of the tangible control exerted over the population as a whole—quite the contrary; but there was a certain relaxation of moral control. To be more precise, the ideological sphere contracted to an appreciable degree, so as to leave room for two forces that were foreign to it by nature, but with which it was able to form a de facto alliance: nationalism (chiefly Great Russian nationalism), and religion (chiefly the Orthodox Church of Moscow). Hence during World War II the Soviet population had the impression—which soon proved a delusion—that it was living under a classic tyranny, and consequently under an infinitely more bearable regime than the mad pseudo reality of the 1930s. The population saw Stalin as a kind of tsar who was particularly cruel, but indispensable to national survival. It put up with surveillance by the Party and police as long as it did not have to take the ideology too seriously, and could live in accordance with the human and traditional passions of patriotic and religious nationalism, or the warrior pleasures of bravery and pillage. The Western statesmen—Churchill, Roosevelt, and De Gaulle—who at the time became acquainted with the Soviet Union shared this point of view. They saw communism as no more than a superficial garment covering the old Russian Empire, which had risen from its ashes, tyrannical and expansionist.

But the ideological regime cannot be transformed into a tyrannical regime without losing its reason for existence, which is to impose pseudo reality by force and to obtain a declaration of allegiance from everyone. I mean that it is not a matter of wringing from the population an agreement for the establishment of "socialism," or its acquiescence in the excellence of the socialist ideal being carried out. The population must declare that socialism has been established, and must demonstrate enthusiasm not for a program, but for a current fulfillment, a result that is considered achieved. Indeed, the ideology sets itself up not only as an ideal to be incarnated but as a law of evolution. It is not morally, but scientifically, true. If, then, the experiment is undertaken in order to prove the law, it is very important that the results be consistent and provide proof.

Take, for example, a kolkhoz. To the eyes of the uninitiated it is, I repeat, a sort of slave plantation, directed by an external bureaucracy and under the surveillance of a system of repression. The serfs receive their food from harvests over which they have no say. They work when ordered to do so; someone else decides what will be sown, what will be plowed or mowed, and so forth. These are not the first plantations in history. They existed under the Roman Empire, in colonial Brazil, in antebellum Virginia. They existed in Russia from the sixteenth century to 1861. But it is very easy to see why an ideological regime—a regime whose ideology is the sort of socialism that took shape in Western Europe during the nineteenth century— cannot recognize a kolkhoz for what it is. To do so would involve a contradiction that would destroy the legitimacy of that ideology.

Nor can such a regime be content with the benevolent passivity, or even the good will, of the kolkhozniki. Suppose that out of patriotism the kolkhozniki, who worked energetically during World War II, had made the following proposal to their masters: "We are serfs, but also patriots. At this moment we want to help you, and we are working almost as ardently as free men in an agricultural co-operative. We consent to tyranny, and we are ready to declare ourselves supporters of socialism, for we cannot but desire the establishment of a regime that bears emblazoned on its banners the workers' right to associate in a freely decided co-operative."

Of course such a proposal would never have been formulated, or even conceived. Nor would it have been accepted by a regime that called itself not potentially but actually socialist. The regime therefore obliged the kolkhoznik to cling to his imaginary position as co-operative farmer, rather than to his real position as serf; to show enthusiasm for irreality, rather than to become resigned to reality; to glory in the present, rather than to hope in the future.

This is why the ideological sphere resumed its expansion immediately after World War II, although tangible constraint was by no means relaxed. The ideological sphere once again invaded the moral realm. If Nicolai Yezhov was the symbol of War Communism II, Andrei Zhdanov became the symbol of War Communism III.

This third War Communism brought the usual inconveniences. New throngs were sent off to the prisons. The economy—or, to avoid that inappropriate term, production —moved along the road to ruin. The widespread brutalization, the enslavement of thought and science, had repercussions upon the war industry and the material resources of Soviet strength. In addition, for peculiar reasons related to Stalin's personality, War Communism could not prevent a certain amount of degeneration in the direction of a classic tyrannical regime.

If, like Aristotle, we define the tyrannical regime as one in which a single man governs in his own personal interest, and the oligarchical regime as one in which an elite governs in its own personal interest, then the Soviet regime is neither a tyranny nor an oligarchy. It governs in the interest of the reality that the ideology presumes to exist—a reality that does not necessarily coincide with the interests of the Party or those of its leader. In 1937 Stalin was able to exterminate the Party not solely for his own personal interest, but for that of the ideology, and on these grounds he had gained the consent of the very individuals he was planning to exterminate. But during the last years of his life Stalin governed by whim, and did not always adhere closely to the unbending coherence of the ideology. He had his favorites, his moods. He assumed the proportions of a big-time gangster rather than an ideologist, and this psychological development—this step toward ordinary humanity—

13

was viewed by his people with tenderness and love, for it is better to live amid crime than madness. But his political behavior was also whimsical and moody. He was leading the Soviet regime to the brink of the abyss. If he had lived a few years longer, that regime might have collapsed.

Stalin died in 1953, and the Party almost immediately decided upon a third NEP. The country was in such a condition that this NEP could only be of long duration. Perhaps sixty million had perished since 1917, if we accept Solzhenitsyn's figure, which seems less and less implausible as information gradually filters through to us. The apparatus of agricultural and industrial production was incapable of assuring the worker that, as Marxists say, his "labor power would be renewed." It also was incapable of providing support for the ambitions of a great power. Khrushchev emptied the concentration camps; he tried to reorganize industry and agriculture; he allowed thought to awaken a bit. The change in atmosphere was enormous. Perhaps never, in its entire history, had the Soviet regime seemed, to foreign and even to Soviet observers, so close to *change*. Yet from a distance the Khrushchev era, or, rather, its beginning, seems to have been a respite, a pause and nothing more.

Solzhenitsyn terms the Khrushchev episode miraculous. That such a corrupt system, such a profoundly criminal Party—a Party that was the product and author of the Great Purge—had placed such a man in the forefront of those in power; that this man, for all his coarseness, could show such human feelings as anger and mirth, and had discovered a personal language with which to express these feelings—this was indeed a miracle as astonishing in its own right as the arrival of Solzhenitsyn himself on the scene.

Khrushchev was nevertheless a Bolshevik. But he was a

Bolshevik in a "naive" way; that is, he thought there was a relationship between a number of values and ideas used by Marxism-Leninism, and the values and ideas commonly known by those same names. So he believed in the universality of the values that Bolshevism claimed to sustain, because he was less caught up than his colleagues in the strict dichotomy of "capitalist" reality and ideological pseudo reality. When he talked of socialism "with butter," he really meant butter to spread on bread. But when, in 1935, Stalin had proclaimed that "life has become better, comrades, life for us has become easier, more joyful," he was simply trying to intimidate through falsification. Khrushchev did not plan to change society, but he wanted socialism to correspond a bit more closely in practice to what it was in theory.

It is not surprising that a program of that sort failed. Pouring money into agriculture could wrest the peasants from physical poverty, make them less unhappy serfs, but they would still be serfs. Khrushchev tried to give Soviet industry the appearance of an industrial economy by granting businesses a certain degree of autonomy, a certain control over purchases, sales, and hiring. He wanted the germ of a market to be developed. He tried to improve accounting and government "planning," and to make them more flexible. For these reforms to succeed, authority relationships would have had to be completely transformed. In the U.S.S.R. the authority in a business is not economic in nature, but political. The mainspring of obedience is not material concerns or monetary gain, but fear of punishment. Economic decisions are made on the same levels as Party decisions, on the local level and on the top level of the Party. As a result, nothing is neutral when it comes to compiling data. It is impossible to establish an accounting

15

system when the results of the computations are supposed to coincide with figures that must be achieved. Administrative level by administrative level, a fictitious statistical structure is created, and from the bottom up artificially reproduces the statistics being handed down by government planners. Nowhere else is ideological pseudo reality obliged to stick so closely to concrete reality, while at the same time having no actual contact with that reality. Under these circumstances, it is impossible to use computers, which are indispensable to comprehensive and efficient government economic planning, for only falsified data could be fed into the machines. This would not be the right approach for eliminating the customary mess.

In intellectual matters, Khrushchev quickly observed that the new tolerance was having little success in winning talented writers or painters over to Leninist "socialism" or to "realism." In this he was sincerely disappointed. Nothing better reveals his deep loyalty to Bolshevism than the resumption of persecution of the Orthodox Church and other sects as well. This persecution was the most violent since the 1930s; perhaps it was a pawn to conciliate the Party.

Among the Party's many reasons for dissatisfaction with Khrushchev were two very important but contradictory ones. For a Bolshevik, Khrushchev was developing a highly personal style of governing that, although it followed a political line contrary to Stalin's, tended, like Stalin's, to make the regime degenerate into a classic tyranny. On the other hand, the Party had reason to fear that he would use the weapons of tyranny to make the Soviet regime side with civil society, that is, with the *common good*. In *The Calf and the Oak** Solzhenitsyn tends to think that Khrushchev, although perhaps not clearly aware of it, was toying

* New York, Association Press, 1975.

with the idea of what would in fact have amounted to a revolution. Deep down, the Party was uncomfortable and felt vaguely threatened. It eliminated him.

The past ten years can be considered among the most flourishing of the Soviet regime. They provide a good example of an apparently successful NEP, characterized by the strengthening of both ideological power and civil society. Let us glance at these two spheres, one after the other.

The two respective spheres were defined in such a way that ideological power maintained firm control over civil society. At the very least, this control by right remained absolute. The peasantry and business apparently fell into step. Ideological language regained all or most of the monopoly it had enjoyed during the most recent phase of War Communism. In this regime where power lies "on the tip of the tongue," the extent to which the "wooden language" spreads is the surest index to the spread of power.

During the Stalin and Khrushchev years, the Bolshevik Party sustained a great loss of personal power, which tended to make the regime evolve into something quite unlike its former self. Since then it has managed to maintain a "collective leadership," which indicates that the First Secretary of the Party is under close enough surveillance by the Politburo and the Central Committee to make sure that his political behavior does not depart unduly from the political behavior enjoying a consensus within the Party. In this sense there is a return to a "state of law" such as the Party may never have known in its long history. At least on the surface, the Party has maintained its unity, which—as it has always known—is the key to remaining in power. The cost of maintaining this state of law is an aging leadership. Most Soviet leaders belong to the generation that assumed power in the brand-new Party that Stalin rebuilt during the purges—the Party rebuilt upon the corpse of the old Party of the 1920s. All of them participated in the operations of that period, all of them purged. A change-over is made difficult by the need to respect the equilibrium established in those days and still in force today.

But power may not find aging leadership a serious drawback. In a well-functioning ideological regime, impersonality is the rule. Once the ideological sphere has been established, its instruments—that is, individuals—are interchangeable. At least that is the ideal. On many occasions this regime has experienced the drawbacks involved in letting an individual develop into a person. The perfect leader is Lenin, who in a remarkable exploit knew how simultaneously to create the revolutionary formula and yet remain the most low-profile, the most elusive of individuals. Impersonality is more easily attainable during middle age. Among young people, ideological asceticism has not yet borne full fruit.

Naiveté, I repeat, consists of granting a universal value to notions that assume their authentic meaning only in the sphere defined by ideology. The naive man, for example, will call a regime where sovereignty belongs to all citizens a democracy, although the latter term should denote a regime where sovereignty belongs to the Communist Party alone; will call an equitable sharing of property among citizens social justice, when the term should mean putting all property at the disposal of the Communist Party alone; will call the autonomy of citizens liberty, when the latter should really refer to the free will of the Communist Party. But *cynicism* constitutes a parallel sort of deviation. It consists of giving a uniquely personal value to ideological notions, or else of applying those notions to everyone else, in order to serve one's personal interest. The cynic, who is aware of the power of ideological language, manipulates it irreproachably, but in private seeks the same pleasures as everyone else: security, wealth, comfort, domination. The right Party line consists of being neither naive nor cynical, but devoted to ideological abstraction just as Lenin was, who did not imagine he had anything in common with those who were not Bolsheviks, and who at the same time was totally disinterested, to the point of not even imagining that for him personal interest existed.

It must be pointed out that, in its deepest core, Lenin's Party was still steeped in naiveté. It must be admitted that Stalin and several of his subordinates had cynical leanings. Khrushchev's Party, hardened in the Leninist and Stalinist school, did not see itself as sharing the fleeting naiveté of its First Secretary. It may be that, in its present form, the Party has lessened these two tensions and achieved a certain homogeneity.

Kostas Papaioannou used the term *cold ideology* for a cooled-down ideology that had lost all power to arouse enthusiasm or even simple belief. At that time (1963–67) he saw cold ideology as a dying ideology, as the end of ideology. But since ideology has maintained its position in the U.S.S.R. and has expanded awesomely in Western Europe and North and South America since 1967, we have reason to ask whether ideology is not at its peak power and effectiveness when it has rid itself of an affectivity, a momentum, born of naiveté, and whether its ultimate form, "the supreme stage of ideology," is not precisely this cold ideology.

Although under Brezhnev the Party is securely protected from naiveté, it certainly is not immune to cynicism. Wherever this deviation was tolerated because it was useful and

19

permitted the formation of a competent elite, subordinate organs such as the army, the diplomatic corps, the police, and the espionage service seem to have been assuming a disproportionate place in the past few years. These organs are amassing all the offensive strength of Bolshevism, are forming its real spearhead. If the Party becomes undistinguishable from the secret police (KGB), it is no longer completely the Party. In the long run, cynical deviation is the most probable, the most threatening deviation. People thoughtlessly speak of "de-Stalinization" when they should say "de-Leninization," for the regime to which this expression is applied is not Stalin's but Lenin's. They do not see to what extent Stalin's regime was actually the first, and until now the most extensive, attempt to de-Leninize. In Eisenstein's film *Ivan the Terrible*—one of the visions of Stalinism personally approved by Stalin—little of the October-born regime is still recognizable. Brezhnev's regime is threatened by the same degeneration, and in prosaic forms that lay no claim to grandeur or the epic. Let us credit him with a sincere return to the Leninist norm; the most methodical return and, on the surface, the most successful in a generation.

The strength of Brezhnev's regime lies in having understood that the ideology no longer was believed. Witnesses all concur in telling us that over there no one "believes" in it. Granted, but they *talk* about it. Before assuming power, the Party obtained cohesion through ideas. Once in power, therefore, it planned to inaugurate an *ideocracy*. But as "real" reality diverged further and further from imaginary reality, ideas became empty and retained only a verbal substance. The regime was evolving into a logocracy.

The *logocracy* assumes an even purer and more supple coherence than the ideocracy. Getting along without internal adherence, it forms a system of action, of behavior, of relationships that nothing can trouble—neither from the outside, because of the police, nor from the inside, because of the disconnecting individual subjectivity. With the exception of those in power, who are obliged to speak the language of the Party cell at home, each individual on his own has uncoupled himself, has disconnected his private life from the system.

Nonetheless, while the void upon which it rests is a calming factor for the ideology, this void at the same time puts the ideology in a precarious position. The ideology presents an unbroken surface, but each rip is harder to mend. It is no longer possible to force dissident literary circles to repent, or to force the author personally to mend the crack his book has opened. The fabric is still intact, carefully maintained, but it is thin, threadbare, worn out.

Now let us turn to civil society, the other component of the pair whose distinctive equilibrium characterizes the post-Stalin NEP.

Granted, the noticeable change that has taken place since 1953 cannot be attributed chiefly to the State, nor have the routinely abortive attempts at agricultural and industrial reform had much effect. The State's role has simply been negative: a relaxation of repression, a decrease in the level of terror, a reduction in the number of people interned, from about ten million to one and a half million, and a need to observe a few semijudicial formalities in making arrests. But that was enough to make civil society revive, which was the goal of the NEP, and to begin to organize itself spontaneously as it saw fit, which the NEP must try to impede.

One of the goals toward which War Communism strives, if it cannot annihilate civil society itself, is to suppress the latter's organicity. Intermediary bodies, natural communities of interest, and groups are destroyed, so that each individual finds himself a solitary atom confronting the State. The U.S.S.R. of 1953 came near to presenting this picture. Twenty-five years later this is no longer the case. What social forces must power reckon with today?

First of all, the *nationalities*. Stalinist War Communism did not manage to humble them to the same degree that it humbled the social classes. In destroying nationalities, Leninist ideology tried to form an alliance with another, less clearly defined ideology: *nationalism,* which plays both a destructive and a preserving role as far as nationalities are concerned. Nationalism is destructive, for it isolates, brutalizes, and morally impoverishes a people that become caught up in it. It brings satisfactions that take the place of liberty. It shatters the human community into hostile groups. In all of this it promotes the workings of the ideology, which move in the same direction. However, there is a threshold beyond which the objective alliance between the principal ideology and the nationalist subideology must break down. Indeed, nationalism binds the national group together, at least in its negative form of a general hatred for other nationalities. It does not easily agree to the destruction of the national group by means other than those stemming from nationalism itself.

As far as nationalism in the U.S.S.R. is concerned, a distinction must be made between the Great Russian nationality on the one hand and all the other nationalities on the other. The Great Russian people had been given the immense satisfaction of being an imperial people. It is just possible that this satisfaction is far superior to those a good government can bestow: prosperity and freedom. Nonetheless, although Russia was the first-born daughter of

Leninist ideology, the latter has not been a good mother. Located at the center of the governmental system and constituting its first instrument, Russia was the first to suffer from the ideology's destructive effects. Ever since the Revolution, Russia's specific gravity in Europe has continually decreased. The demographic gap—deaths, plus a low birth rate compared with the rate forecast by demographers—runs to over a hundred million. The Russian people, who on the eve of World War I seemed destined to outnumber the German population, are scarcely any larger in number today, although history has not been kind to the Germans either. The Russians are now a tired, aging, demographically stagnant people. In addition, despite an intense program of Russification, the relative weight of the Russians within the U.S.S.R. is decreasing.

Consequently, a degree of discontent is being shown by Great Russian nationalism, which sees its imperial role threatened. Amenable to any regime whatsoever—even one that destroys authentically Russian values—provided such a regime assures it peaceful domination over the peoples that surround it, Great Russian nationalism may well be hoping for a different regime that can offer just such an assurance. The alliance between nationalism and Leninism, which was so decisive in Bolshevism's conquest of the planet, may no longer be as strong in Russia as it once was.

The other nations that form the major part of the U.S.S.R. share an irreconcilable hatred for the Russian nation. This hatred constitutes the most active, most conscious, and most offensive force in their basic anti-Soviet feelings—feelings that remain latent through indifference, lassitude, and habit.

Where are the national movements today? Judging them by the magnitude of militant nationalism could lead to errors in perspective. In the Ukraine, about which a certain amount of information is available, a string of tiny groups continually keeps forming and then reforming. The Soviet government apparently has no trouble breaking them up and sending them off to concentration camps. Periodically the movement has its most active militants skimmed off in this way. The same is true, it seems, in the Baltic countries. The Jewish people have the advantage of possessing an effective foreign base—doubtless more actively supportive than the foreign bases also available to the Ukrainians and Armenians. Above all, the Jewish people have not set up for themselves national goals within the framework of the U.S.S.R.; their goal is emigration. But the fact that they achieve it, albeit in extremely modest numbers, serves as a resonance box for the other national demands, and can only encourage the formation of militant local units.

A better test would be resistance to Russification. There is effective resistance in the Turkic regions, where cultural, ethnic, and religious barriers are especially strong. These regions adjoin one another geographically. There the rapidly increasing population has remained on the spot, and is said to be rejecting foreign influences. Toward the West—in the Ukraine, for example—resistance is more difficult. The teaching of—and in most cases *in*—Russian strikes a sympathetic chord in regions where moral or cultural ties with the Great Russian people have long existed. Throughout the U.S.S.R., the Russians form compact and of course privileged groups in the midst of other peoples. Should Soviet power weaken, abrupt and almost immediate secessions would surely occur. Displacement and massive deportation—for which the Soviet government has provided an example and shown the feasibility—would be the probable fate of those Russians scattered throughout the territories of other ethnic groups.

Of all the problems the Soviet government must face, the national problem is the most insoluble, and the only one that in the long run seems fatal to it, the only one that in the long run will cause the demise, if not of communism, at least of the political ensemble that is the U.S.S.R. For sixty years the government has employed every possible means to ward off this danger. It balkanized the Turkic countries. It created a superficial federalism. It Russified. It colonized. It deported the peoples with the smallest populations. Stalin lamented that there were so many Ukrainians that even the most intrepid administrator of the Gulag would lose heart. At the time of his death he had already built camps in Siberia to confine the Jews. He tried to channel local nationalism into parochialism and into an extremely artificial folk tradition, in his desire to sublimate it totally into a fleeting "Soviet patriotism." None of it worked, and the nations still exist. The government has up its sleeve a plan for redefining internal boundaries that disregards national frontiers and is based upon imaginary "economic regions," whereby every foot of the Ukraine or Lithuania would become incorporated into a large territory peopled by Russians. The project presupposes a transformation in the Soviet constitution. Since that constitution has never had any but a fictitious existence, this appears easy; but national feeling is so deeply rooted that such a step seems too daring, and the government keeps backing off.

Closely linked to the national rebirth is the religious rebirth. Over the two-part division I proposed for nationalism, we can superimpose another two-part division, between the Orthodox Church of the Patriarch of Moscow and the other faiths.

Except during World War II and during the moral NEP, which sought a very close alliance between the regime and all the remaining forces of civil society, the Orthodox Church has been subjected to the longest and most intense persecution in recorded history, exclusive of the persecution of the Catholic Church in Japan during the seventeenth century. Unlike Japan, Russia had been Christian for a thousand years. The Church has been decimated, since most bishops and priests, accompanied by many of the faithful, have been sent off to the camps. The Church has been corrupted, for many priests collaborate with the police, when they are not police agents themselves. Although the State expresses its intention to destroy the Church, and announces that it will not settle for mere submission, the hierarchy is demonstrating the same exemplary docility toward the new regime that characterized it during the old one.

The golden rule of repression consists of pushing it to the exact point at which the faithful will desert the Church in large numbers, whether to enter the world of sects, to create a schism, or to withraw into an inner piety. However, this entails the disadvantage of removing these faithful from the strict control to which they are subject within the framework of the established parishes.

Employing this rule is ticklish. First of all, within the void that gapes behind the ideological façade, a rebirth of religious feeling and observance has been noted, and even a rebirth of the religious intellectual and philosophical life. If the rule mentioned is to be applied, the threshold of tolerance must be raised. The interrelationship between religious life and national life also plays its part. The rebirth of the values of the former means the rebirth of the values of the latter. Among the intelligentsia, thinking and being free again to read the national classics means entering a Christian framework of thought.

Below the official Orthodox Church, in Russian regions, lies the confused and poorly understood world of the schismatics and sectarians. Despite even harsher repression than that inflicted upon the patriarchal church, this world persists and expands to the degree that it can feed upon the mortal remains of the Orthodox Church. This is also the case for the baptist movement.

Elsewhere one might generalize that it is difficult to distinguish the religious question from the national question: the Uniates of the Ukraine, the Catholics and Lutherans of the Baltic countries, the Monophysites of Armenia, the Jews, and the Moslems—all suffer twice, once as believers and once as peoples.

The ideological regime has always been uncomfortable about dealing with the national and religious phenomena that do not fit into its classifications. It had a hard time cutting down those intangible things whose existence it did not even understand. The subjection of the social classes was an easier and more clear-cut matter.

The pulverization of the working class was in every respect a model operation. Indeed, it was there that the false ideology—the instrumental substitution of an imaginary reality for reality—could be imposed with maximum effectiveness. At the beginning, the working class was praised messianically. Somewhat later, the Party was considered to be acting in its name and place, through a permanent and mystically justified delegation of authority. Since the working class as an eschatological entity no longer "inhabited" the social group composed of manual laborers in factories, the latter were immediately deprived of all their rights and soon came to be considered the servants of the "working class," whose soul, by metempsychosis, had transmigrated into the Party apparatus. The soviets acted as rather informal, spontaneous strike committees, incapable of replacing the union organization that had been sabotaged by the Bolsheviks. The soviets were Bolshevized as early as July 1918. "Syndicate" was the name chosen by the branch of the State police specializing in the surveillance of factory workers. Piecework; workers' papers that were infinitely more detailed than those of French workers during the Restoration; fines and prison sentences for the slightest infraction of work rules; and a huge drop in wages—these were a few of the conditions peculiar to a Soviet worker under Stalin.

At the beginning of Khrushchev's NEP the Soviet worker's position was worse than that of any worker in the history, and even prehistory, of Western capitalism. With no organization, no right to strike, no benefit funds, it is not surprising that a working class—in the sense given that term by nineteenth-century sociologists—no longer existed in Russia. Only the category of manual workers in factories still existed. The working class no longer existed, except in the pseudo reality of banners, May Day parades, and the names of newspapers.

The working world had so totally lost its identity that it became the segment of the Soviet population we know least about; we have a splendid detailed knowledge of life in prisons and camps, but not in factories. Yet certain evidence assembled during the past twenty years leads us to think that this working world has invented a number of ways of fighting and organizing. Strikes have been reported. Although put down by machine guns, they have forced the authorities to take certain precautions. It seems that workers are now in a position to influence their working and living conditions. Through absenteeism, slow-down strikes, cautious sabotage, and theft, they are obtaining higher wages and supplementary benefits.

The same is true for the peasants. Confined to plantations, compelled to do forced labor, they have been reduced to beggary. More numerous than all the peasants of Western Europe and North America, they are incapable of producing enough to feed the country from the most extensive and fertile lands in the world. War Communism I was not able to crush the peasant world. NEP I allowed it to heal itself spontaneously. War Communism II once again brought the peasantry back under control and within the sphere of ideological power, but at the price of an agricultural catastrophe. The miraculous unproductivity of the Russian peasant is an index of both this control and its failure. In theory, control was not relaxed during NEP III. On the contrary, the government contemplated resolving the crisis by a dramatic tightening of control. It was planned to destroy the village and the *isba,* or log hut, and thus the traditional manner of organizing fields, and to deport the entire peasantry to a reduced number of living units, so as to force it to increase productivity within a previously planned new setting. This plan has not been abandoned, but it has not been put into force either. In this case, peasant society showed its capacity for resistance.

Peasants and workers draw their strength from the existence of the market. Even in the midst of the various War Communisms, the market could not be suppressed. The kolkhoz market is the free or black market made official. What is improperly called the official or State market is an arbitrary and capricious distribution of items at arbitrary prices in return for arbitrary remuneration. The surest sign of the increasing strength of civil society during the past twenty-five years is the astounding growth of the market. First there is the agricultural products market. Here the kolkhoz market has a twin: a widespread black market organized by the peasants. It appears that many kolkhozy, especially in the various ethnic Republics, are fictitious kolkhozy existing only on paper; that is, instead of being slave plantations adorned with the name "collective farms" (in Russian, *kolkhozy*), these are authentic collective ventures, something like peasant co-operatives, which try to look like slave plantations to the administration.

Also there is the labor market, where one finds workers' pressure upon pay, black-market labor, double and triple wages, and utilization of State-owned material for private commercial purposes. And lastly, the business market. Indeed, to achieve the objectives of the government plan on paper (using falsified bookkeeping), businesses are forced to procure raw materials, workers, as well as replacement parts on the widespread black market. The whole network of State stores selling manufactured goods, and raw or semi-finished materials, is integrated into the network of financial transactions based upon a price established by mutual consent. Even gold has a market price. In other words, alongside the Soviet noneconomy is a real economy that corresponds to the standard definition of an economy: a rational management of scarcity, expressed in accounting terms. But this economy is not official; it exists outside the law and cannot use public measuring devices. So it is clandestine, illegal, and primitive, resembling sometimes the vast Arab trade at the time of the *Arabian Nights,* sometimes the trade of the Chinese compradors, and sometimes the deals concluded by the American Mafia and the activities of the Cosa Nostra in New York and Chicago. As such, it generates a considerable part of the national wealth, and permits the official system of production to function.

After this rapid summary of the positions of civil society and power, a few words must be said about an intermediary group, the intelligentsia. Viewed historically, the intelligentsia can be considered a creation of the State, which needed a category of personnel trained by it and able to carry out general tasks requiring greater specialization than that of technicians and foremen. But it also can be considered a reflection of civil society, to the degree that it attempts to assert its rights and autonomy vis-à-vis the State. The upper intelligentsia of the Old Regime was promptly eliminated by the Bolshevik leadership. But this leadership itself had been profoundly infiltrated by the middle and lower intelligentsia, although, within the framework of the Party, it had lost its identity as intelligentsia. If it attempted to resume that identity, it would once more be in the ambiguous position just described.

At the end of the Stalinist period, the intelligentsia found itself in a strange situation. With the exception of a few individuals, its best members had gone off to the camps, never to return. The rest felt sufficiently endangered to permit the State to hold over their heads the threat of a pogrom by the people. But if the intelligentsia had to fear the "people" as much as it feared the State, and if, in a sense, it found protection in the State, even so in another sense it was in the "people," in civil society, that it found refuge and protection from the State. During the NEPs the intelligentsia, working for its own autonomy, expanded its horizons. To its official function as engineer of souls, it added the traditional functions of expressing the human conscience, and moreover protected the souls it was supposed to be shaping.

The restoration of the Russian intelligentsia since Stalin betrays the wear and tear in the ideological fabric. The greatest threat that the intelligentsia poses to power lies in its voicing, alongside the wooden language, a human language, one that is essentially just that: human. Indeed, the communist regime begins when the people (the State) expropriates, not the means of production, but the means of communication. Long before factories and fields were seized, newspapers, presses, the media had been confiscated. This had already occurred by November 8, 1917, when the authority of the regime did not reach beyond the limits of Petrograd, if even that far. A much more immediate and deadly threat than a restored market is the threat of restored human speech, the private use of the vocal cords, the individual ownership of the throat. Even before knowing what a writer is writing about, the censors sense his tone, the way in which he says it. This is why, according to Efim Etkind, the first of the thirteen censors who must approve any given text is a stylistic censor. The editor rewrites the text to make it conform to the rhetorical patterns of the wooden language. The censors grasped all the implications of Buffon's statement that style is the man.

Once the stylistic barrier has been crossed, the rest is a matter of course. The writer breaks the pact of lies upon which the entire equilibrium of ideological power rests. He restores the correct meanings to words. He rights the ideological inversion of the language. He re-establishes reality as the only reality, and volatilizes pseudo reality. Then—though this can be considered almost secondary—he makes public the facts that the censors wanted to hide. Finally, he demands the return of law and denounces injustice.

All these functions have been brilliantly performed by the Russian intelligentsià during the past twenty-five years. We need only cite the names of Boris Pasternak, Anna Akhmatova, Nadezhda Mandelstam, Alexander Solzhenitsyn, Andrei Amalrik, and Andrei Sakharov. The intelligentsia could not be content to play the role of justice. In order to create, it also must restore the culture, and resolder the links of a long interrupted cultural continuity. But in so doing, it finds itself cornered by various choices that threaten its unity. As we know, the current chart of the intelligentsia is an exact reproduction of the gamut of trends that existed under the Old Regime. Some are going back to the old "official nationalism" of the Great Russian imperial tradition; others, through religion, have returned to slavophilism; still others, focusing upon democracy and freedom, are espousing Westernism.

Yet a great number of intellectuals have not gone that far. Scholars, high-level technicians, and managers, they simply want to use their skills and work effectively without having to pay tribute to ideology. The latter seems to them an absurd survival, for they do not understand that ideology forms one body with the regime, or, rather, itself constitutes the regime. It is this segment of the intelligentsia that is closest to civil society, which is spontaneously apolitical and concerned only with its own development.

For a logocratic regime, the existence of an intelligentsia that has become the bearer of free speech is per se intolerable. Until now, however, the government has succeeded in isolating it within strict limits. The dissemination of forbidden works has been restricted. According to Sakharov, this is the reason behind most of the purely political prison sentences. Except in Moscow and Leningrad, or in certain ethnic Republics, the ponderous Soviet lack of information reigns everywhere. In addition, there is as yet no connection between intellectual dissidents and the vague popular discontent. This discontent is being expressed through alcoholism, anti-Semitism, chauvinism, and delinquency. It has not yet found political expression. Sakharov tallies only five to ten thousand purely political prisoners among what he estimates to be a million and a half detainees (compared to about fifty thousand in 1913). The other detainees—that is, almost all of them: nationalists, religious believers, thieves, black marketeers—are the product of a civil society that is being reconstituted; they have simply gone beyond the limits permitted by the NEP.

Depending upon the condition of civil society, there is either an NEP or War Communism. On the cultural level, there has been no NEP since 1922, when what I have called the NEP first began. On the political level, there has been no NEP since the beginning of rural collectivization.

Next, let us note one thing: the couple formed by the regime and society has remained intact. By its very nature Bolshevik power—which is devoted to a reality different from that of its subjects, and sees things in terms only of this reality—cannot "emanate" from civil society. For it to emanate from that society would require a revolution which, by abolishing pseudo reality, would give power to ordinary reality. The nature of that power would henceforth be totally different, if it even remained tyrannical. It is clear that since the time of Stalin's death—a very long time, in any epoch of history—the nature of the Soviet regime has not changed. Indeed, it has not changed since November 7, 1917—an unheard-of performance among modern regimes. What has changed is the U.S.S.R., which as a reality remains within history and keeps pace with it. But, having been based upon pseudo reality, the regime as a result escapes history. Consequently it cannot be corrupted, for corruption is down-to-earth. The regime lies within the sphere of the unchanging. It can only disappear, or perpetuate itself indefinitely.

It was with a view to self-perpetuation that the regime chose between the two policies of War Communism and the NEP. It could be shown that, before gaining power, Lenin invented these two policies as general tactics and attitudes to use upon the opposition and future allies, thus forming inalterable molds into which the specific contents of War Communism and NEP later were poured. Lenin also established the two extreme limits that neither of these two tactics must exceed, and beyond which the Party risked siding either with leftism, sectarianism, adventurism, or with rightism, opportunism, "liquidationism." What, then, is the correct party line? Depending upon which of the two tactical directions has been chosen, it consists of preserving the possibility, the freedom, for the Party to backtrack as soon as it decides to do so. War Communism and the NEP are only valid to the degree they are *reversible*. If by mischance the Party were to let itself be carried away, so that it could no longer control developments and, by subordinating everything to the supreme criterion of preserving its power, order an *about-face*, it would be sure to lose that power rapidly and be destroyed.

This, then, is the dilemma that the Soviet government must face: should we continue the NEP, or should we move on to War Communism? The dilemma is not a new one. It must have arisen in 1964, at the time of Khrushchev's disgrace, which brought an instant halt to an NEP that was threatening to get irreversibly out of control. Since then the government has been feeling its way and has maintained a precarious equilibrium, which nonetheless is a continuation of the NEP, since civil society organizes and strengthens itself spontaneously, if not subjected to violent duress. Whenever the government stops taking the initiative, it must pay concerted attention to maintaining the Party apparatus intact, to putting a brake on society's spontaneous initiative. It therefore plays a conservative role. This is why Soviet and foreign observers use the terms "reactionary" or "conservative" to describe the governing group, which behaves as it does for defensive reasons, but with the intention of maintaining intact its "revolutionary" ideological capability, in oder to deploy it in other circumstances.

But can the government let matters take their course and continue a de facto NEP? Here we must cast theoretical speculations aside and look closely at what is going on. It seems that, since early 1975, the regime has been moving decisively toward a major political about-face. We can at least understand why. If things go on as they are, civil society may gain so much credit that it would become decisively stronger than the Party. The chief indication of this would be that, instead of remaining intact within ideological pseudo reality, the Party would be invaded by the powerful currents of reality and would be influenced by them; it would be devoured from the inside or digested by reality. And so the Party would more or less mirror national hostilities. There would be Ukrainian, Russian, Caucasian clans. Or social conflicts would be reflected: various elements would be watching out for the interests of cities, rural areas, business leaders, or technicians. Or else the Party might enter the market economy and allow itself to be corrupted. In this case, corruption would not have a pejorative meaning, for although the corruption of the best is the worst thing of all, the corruption of the worst is the best thing of all.

The Party already has increased its own material privileges considerably over the years, but it has insisted that the circuit of consumer goods and special remuneration, from which it is the sole to profit, be maintained outside the parallel market. This has meant creating a special network of stores, accessible only to the Party, and, to ward off temptation, an accounting system based on hand-to-hand cash payments. But temptation, like cupidity, is infinite. Sakharov reports that the courts have taken to accepting bribes. The pressure of the market is felt everywhere. The natural—but not communist—desire to form a privileged, hereditary caste involves a virtual sale of offices. Numerous accounts condemn the increasing venality within the educational system, especially in the award of diplomas. When the offspring of a communist family lacks sufficient merit to assure admission to the university or one of the special institutes, one is tempted to resort to the black market in advanced degrees and doctorates. But the general drift toward cynicism, so strong in the Communist Party today, does not prevent the Party from also being exposed to the opposite deviation: naiveté. Indeed, among the children of government figures —children who have been given privileges unknown to the rest of the population—a querulous mood, and the standard signs of rebellion, can be observed. Among this group the dissident intellectuals find recruits, accomplices, and protectors.

But can there be a return to War Communism? In a communist system it is a touchy matter to govern subtly; the natural tendency is to go to extremes. This is what occurred during each of the about-faces where the regime either moved toward or backed off from War Communism. But this did not happen during the about-face that began in 1964 and that has remained only a semi-about-face—perhaps through the wishes of the governing, but even more surely through necessity, that is, through impotence. For here lies the heart of the debate: *Does the government have the political means to effect a clear-cut return to War Communism?*

Indeed, what does such a return mean? In a word, it means *repression*. In order to crush civil society, in order to prune off the shoots that have sprouted during the past twenty-five years, vast purges must be carried out.

The obstacles are not moral ones. In the U.S.S.R. the people know from experience that the State can do anything. The State is bound by nothing except the duties imposed upon it by ideology, and these duties are not related to civil society. One of the differences between the classic tyranny and the ideological regime is that the tyrant, who seeks his own interests, is still linked with the common interest, and that he is ruined by the ruin of his subjects. The tyrant, who is a cynic and who remains within the same reality as his subjects, can carry out inquiries and make lucid decisions. And so the Mongol khans would judge with an open mind whether a certain region of the Empire should be transformed into pastures for grazing horses, or whether it would be more advantageous to collect tribute from the inhabitants. By way of contrast, up until the very last moment—the moment of its final collapse—ideological pseudoreality is unaffected by the destruction of real reality. This is because the Party is convinced that it is merely transferring reality's wealth to pseudoreality, as in those science-fiction stories where objects and people disintegrate and disappear, while being transported intact into the "fourth dimension." It takes time to realize that the fourth dimension does not exist, and that the objects and people have simply vanished into nothingness.

The obstacles are political ones. In theory, the purge should have two phases. First it should strike the Party itself. In a regime where political life is monopolized by the Party, every change is expressed by a change in the Party. In a regime where a political error is simultaneously a moral error and an ontological defect, the change in the Party is expressed through the political death of a fraction of the Party—a fraction, however, that can be almost as extensive as the Party itself. Since political death is an ontological annihilation, there are no inconveniences in its going hand in hand with physical death. On the contrary, such a death provides a shortcut to maintaining the monolithic unity of the Party, and unity has always been acknowledged as the basic condition for its survival. In addition, political death offers the advantage of making careers and posts available for countless subordinates whose promotion has been blocked. The Soviet Party is under the thumb of the gerontocracy and remains immobile; as in Stalin's day, the purge would bring rejuvenation and an opportunity to ensure the succession of the next generation in the traditional manner.

Nonetheless, the purge is a dangerous political venture; it is hard to keep under control. The generation in power knows this from experience: the changing of the guard may not go as planned. In 1936 there was a combination of cynicism and naiveté of a sort no longer found today, for naiveté has become a scarce commodity. Then too, in 1936 civil society had just been crushed, and the operation could be conducted in peace. Is this true today? Would not repression

39

be necessary in both the Party and civil society? And with such risks!

For the chief phase of the purge obviously involves civil society. Crush the peasantry once more? Carry out the ultimate deportation, the deportation not merely of the kulaks but of the entire village? This would provoke a famine at least comparable to those of 1921 and 1932. Cut down the working class? But how then would production be maintained? Annihilate the market? Would the Soviet economy still be capable of supplying the State with the needed instruments of military force? And how can the national problem be solved without resorting to methods that made Stalin himself recoil—Stalin, who hesitated to deport the Jews and the Ukrainians?

It is not certain that Stalin's methods derived from his personal characteristics. In large part, they stemmed from the nature of the undertaking to be carried out within the framework of the existing political system. The same operation, within the same political system, but applied on a hitherto unknown scale, would involve a corresponding increase in the level of human costs. If War Communism II cost at least thirty million dead, how much would War Communism IV cost? Solzhenitsyn wisely observed that it would mean the end of the historic existence of the Russian people.

A State Unlike Any Other

At this point we come to foreign policy. Do we find in it political patterns that correspond to those encountered in domestic policy? What policy should be adopted in order to create an international environment conducive to the domestic aims anticipated during these about-faces?

By foreign policy I mean the activities of the Soviet Communist Party beyond the official boundaries of the U.S.S.R. This policy is characterized by the fact that it has two systems of action which, for convenience, I shall call System A and System B.

These two systems correspond to the two spheres—ideological pseudo reality and ordinary reality—discussed above.

System A is related to the ideological sphere, in which nations are not considered permanent and unyielding components of foreign policy. One might even say that, within this sphere, the notion of foreign policy loses its substance, since the point of reference is on the one hand world capitalism, and on the other the international communist movement. Foreign policy therefore exists only as a result of historical and temporary circumstances. The working concepts of System A are drawn from the doctrine. For example, they include imperialism, class struggle on the international scale, and proletarian internationalism. The means employed by System A—at least those that are its very own —are the international communist movement, particularly its specialized organs: the Comintern, the Cominform, the World Federation of Trade Unions, etc. Working alongside these organs are more unobtrusive apparatuses such as those that carry out, within the "fraternal" communist parties, the information, propaganda, and subversive services, and other functions assigned to the KGB and similar organs.

System B develops upon close contact with ordinary reality or, more exactly, along the offensive front or the moving frontier that separates the ideological sphere from real reality. Here it is a question of a foreign policy in the usual sense of the term: an inter-state policy. The working concepts are taken from the traditional diplomatic vocabulary. Thus within System B are heard such words as peace, coexistence, national sovereignty, nonintervention in the internal affairs of other countries, influence, and special interests. The means employed by System B are, as everywhere else, diplomacy, the army, economic exchanges, and all other means by which one state can act upon another.

System B is linked to System A to the precise degree that ideology is in power and, without letting go, keeps under its thumb a portion of reality that has the appearance of a state. In practice, both systems were put into operation simultaneously and inseparably. The policy of the Communist Party of the U.S.S.R. and the policy of the U.S.S.R. are continuously connected and interacting.

It would be erroneous to imagine, as people sometimes seem to do, that during offensive periods in foreign policy System A is dominant, and during defensive periods, System B. If so, according to this theory the foreign policy of the Communist Party—a revolutionary policy—would gradually fade away in favor of a traditional state policy that may be expansionist, but that is striving to become part of the community and, soon after that, part of the concert of powers.

In actual practice foreign policy, when on the offensive, makes use of all the state-controlled powers that are part of System B, just as, when on the defensive, it uses the more unobtrusive resources of System A. The art of Soviet foreign policy involves combining the two systems of action so that they do not hamper each other, and reach full effectiveness within their respective contexts. Lenin understood immediately that the second system could not exist without the first. Just as the supreme rule for domestic policy is to remain in power, so the rule for foreign policy is to preserve at all costs the State's rank and ability to act. The most extreme, and also the most exemplary, application of this rule was the acceptance—despite the disapproval of Trotsky and the majority of the Politburo—of the conditions of the Brest-Litovsk Treaty. Trampling on what, in System B, would be called national interests, Lenin accepted the amputation of half of Russia in order to retain control of a territory with status as a state.

The State is therefore seen as a position to fall back to, a place of refuge where the international communist movement finds shelter whenever it is in difficulty. And international communism can be mobilized to defend the State. In that case, instead of its own language—imperialism, class struggle, proletarian internationalism—System A begins to speak the language of System B. It is also bilingual, as indicated by the title of the Cominform newspaper during the 1950s. During those years foreign policy could be categorized as offensive in Eastern Europe and defensive in Western Europe, so the newspaper was called *For a Lasting Peace* (B), *For a People's Democracy* (A). This was also the period of the Stockholm Peace Appeal (System A for means, B for vocabulary), the Korean War, and the Berlin blockade (System B), when the international communist movement was entrusted with the tactical defense, while the offensive strategy was put in the hands of the Soviet State and its military capabilities. But even this is too simple: constantly, whatever offensive or defensive political line has been chosen, the two systems act simultaneously by employing, according to the place and the circumstances, every means of attack and defense, since, as in war, defense can be the best attack and attack the surest defense.

As long as the ideology has not been expressly repudiated, the general orientation of Soviet foreign policy will be offensive. This is why I do not believe that the concepts "offensive" and "defensive" are operative here and sufficient to categorize Soviet foreign policy by periods. They are only valid within a tactical and local context, for the strategy is basically offensive. Indeed, ideological pseudo reality will not become less intense until it has entirely absorbed the reality under its control; nor will it be satisfied with its territory or feel secure until its frontiers are identical with those of the Universe. Any result obtained within System B and ratified in the fashion of that system, once rethought and retranscribed into the categories of System A, will be considered temporary and cannot be given firm ratification. "What is ours is ours, what is yours is negotiable." What is ours belongs to us according to the canons of ideology, while according to the same canons, what is yours does not belong to you and should by rights revert to us.

So what good are treaties?

From the very earliest months of the new regime, the

government noted the advantages to be gained from the fundamental contrast between its own foreign policy and that of its partners. The latter are prepared only to act and think within System B. They can therefore easily misconstrue a diplomacy that feels very free to use System B since, ontologically speaking, it does not take that system seriously. A treaty is never a settlement, which might strive for equity and hence satisfy both sides. It is the official statement of a power relationship in a conflict that, by nature, excludes compromise and desires the final defeat of one of the two partners.

But this statement is *formulated.* That is, it obliges the adversary (for no partner exists) to express in precise terms his explicit gratitude for a situation and a reality, and this gratitude immediately becomes an asset for pseudo reality. And so pseudo reality in a way becomes imbued with reality —not only the controlled reality, but also the reality it does not control. Pseudo reality is made official and is given an apparent existence by its irreducible enemy, who, as soon as the treaty is signed, falls into the thought patterns of pseudo reality. In this way every treaty between the United States and the U.S.S.R. is transformed into a treaty—in this instance, a simple snapshot of a temporary situation—between capitalism and socialism. By the linking concept of "peaceful coexistence," the United States itself accepts this transformation: it officially accepts being the representative of capitalism and letting the U.S.S.R. represent socialism. And so in recent years the socialism-capitalism dichotomy —a dichotomy that has meaning only within the ideology —has gradually been accepted by various national public opinions and by the European press.

The great powers that negotiate with the U.S.S.R., and think within the framework of System B, believe that a concrete agreement involving frontiers, merchandise, or armaments constitutes the only reality, and that they are not affected by concessions, which are made within the nonbilateral framework of System A. These are unimportant, unreal verbal satisfactions that can be given to the Soviet government to gain its good will. But the great powers are mistaken. The ideology is a verbal system that is based upon, and feeds upon, words. Giving it words, yielding to it in matters of words, means conferring upon it the only reality it can have. In its domestic governing, the Party is not satisfied with simple obedience; it wants an acquiescence, a confession, an expressed assent. In foreign policy, the treaty is the equivalent of the confession in a court of law, or the assent in a unanimous vote. The treaty does not ratify a division, it ratifies the legitimacy of the imaginary and the recognition of the nonexistent. The verbal concession becomes a negation of the legitimacy of the one who has made the concession, and this concession is immediately used against him. The wreath of flowers that the French President Giscard d'Estaing laid at Lenin's mausoleum was not an insignificant act. Giscard d'Estaing justified it by asserting that he was laying that wreath in homage to the founder of the Soviet State, and so in a sense he remained within the framework of System B. Yet, in fact, he was depositing the wreath at the feet of the founder of the international communist movement.

It would be equally incorrect to imagine, as people sometimes do, that the War Communism phases coincide with "offensive" phases, and the NEP phases with "defensive" phases, of foreign policy. A quick look at the past would show, on the contrary, that these two rhythms appear to be independent of each other. Marshal Tukhachevsky's raid in

Poland occurred in the midst of War Communism, but so did Stalin's prudent behavior vis-à-vis Hitler and Truman. On the other hand, subversive efforts in Germany in 1923 and in China belong to the NEP.

The greatest successes of Soviet foreign policy occurred during the long period since Stalin's death, and especially since Khrushchev's fall. It has become a cliché to say that the West won the Cold War but lost détente. But we might well ask ourselves whether, as a general rule, the NEP at home is not more conducive to an active foreign policy than War Communism is.

Indeed, according to our definition, War Communism implies that the forces of the Communist Party are focused upon civil society, that is, upon domestic affairs. It needs a tranquil international climate in order peacefully to carry out its principal business. Therefore its foreign policy—which can moreover include tactical aspects that are very offensive and "revolutionary"—will basically attempt to maintain the status quo. We shall return to this point. In addition, the partial destruction of civil society deprives the Party of the means for a truly active foreign policy. Its army must rely upon an exhausted economy, upon a technology lacking in initiative. Lastly, news of the extensive repression cannot be concealed behind the high walls of secrecy, and such news triggers a certain fear in international society. The international communist movement is therefore not always in a favorable position.

On the other hand the NEP, which implies a partial and temporary retreat from the domestic tasks of the Communist Party, nonetheless frees the Party for foreign tasks. And so the Party takes on a relatively liberal appearance. Western opinion, which is easily satisfied, throws open its arms, and the remnant of secrecy becomes an extra spice, an *aura*

49

that permits all the ensuing overevaluations. It is easier for Western Communist Parties to be unitary if they do not have to face up to such scandals as the 1936 trials or those that followed the Tito affair.

Last, and most important, the Party benefits from civil society's recovered strength. Now let us turn to the army.

"War," Lenin was fond of saying (quoting Clausewitz out of context), "is politics carried out by other means." The interesting thing about that sentence coming from Lenin is not the meaning given to the word "war," but the meaning of the word "policy." Indeed, in Lenin's Manichaean vision policy cannot lead to an equitable division among social groups or among the cities that share the Universe. It is an over-all dramatic confrontation in which one party must win a total victory and the other be eliminated. Policy is therefore inclined to go to extremes, in other words, to war. The difference between policy and war becomes a purely technical matter, with war using different material means from those employed by policy—means that usually are more costly. At any rate, a policy must foresee war and prepare the means to carry it out. Therefore, since policy in a communist regime is wholly defined as the acquisition and perpetuation of power on both local and world levels, the government gives priority to the task of building an army capable of securing world power and of paving the way for local control.

The army is the true aim of the Soviet system of production. From the government's point of view and from that of the ideological sphere—the only sphere to which the government is accountable—it makes little difference whether civil society is prosperous or impoverished. As a civil society it has no share in power, and the government is not afraid of being overthrown by a nationwide show of discontent. Since it is outside the ideological sphere, it has no legitimate existence of its own. It is not the peasant as such who is supposed to be well off, or even the plantation adorned with the title of kolkhoz, to which the peasant is enslaved; rather, it is the kolkhoz as it exists in the imagination, in a utopia— that is to say, nowhere.

Since investments and research are determined by political imperatives, it is not surprising that they are not dedicated to the well-being of civil society. As we know, not one single medicine, not one single useful consumer product, has been invented in the U.S.S.R. during the past sixty years. Medicine and pharmacopoeia remain at an extraordinarily primitive level, and there are few countries where plumbing facilities are as "underdeveloped." It is hard to imagine something that would motivate the Soviet system of production to invent and then perfect an electric razor or a washing machine. The army, on the contrary, is the central preoccupation. At most, the government's sole duty, as far as the production of items for civil society is concerned, is to permit that society to attain a standard of living that will enable it to support the push for military production. There are, of course, electric razors and washing machines in the U.S.S.R., but they are copied from foreign models, thus freeing labor for truly productive—in other words, military—tasks.

Productive effort is more concentrated in the military industries in the U.S.S.R. than in any other country in the world. The official figures have little meaning. Certain Western specialists estimate that the portion of the GNP spent on defense—between ten and twenty percent—is twice as great as in the United States. Sakharov says it is forty percent, a higher percentage than is spent on armaments in Israel, a nation that is constantly prepared for war. Anyone

51

using these figures must be fully aware that Soviet statistics are dubious. In addition, we know that a vast amount of research, talent, and scientific equipment has been earmarked for the military sector.

It is a matter of fact that, since the Revolution, the Soviet State has managed to build a competitive army. The problem of building a modern army based on a relatively primitive economy was solved by the concentration of resources, by coercion, and by lowering or raising the standard of living. This has been the time-tested approach ever since Peter the Great. But there is another condition, an unusual one, that has enabled the U.S.S.R. to reach equivalence in this domain. In the U.S.S.R. the military sector is the only one that must heed the rational criteria that, in noncommunist countries, determine the over-all system of production. It makes little difference whether the products of civil industry are very inferior in quality to those produced abroad. Who will complain if the Soviet population is dressed in bargain-basement fashions and eats the sort of food served in soup kitchens? But the regime cannot afford to have poor quality planes, tanks, and artillery. Since there is no true market, which would imply a calculation of production costs just as impossible in this sector as in the others, it is competition or rivalry that imposes quality and compels innovation. The military sector is the only sector of the economy that, in this roundabout way, experiences the stimulation of the market.

This circumstance must be taken into account when interpreting the enormous mushrooming of the Soviet armed forces. Indeed, it is difficult to decide whether this expansion always results from a carefully weighed policy aimed at military action and reflecting a decision of the chiefs of staff. Or does this mushrooming come about through a sort of automatism and built-in destiny, as if it were an offshoot of the peculiar Soviet system of production, naturally oriented toward things military, equipped and effective in this sector alone? If this is so, the U.S.S.R. is producing tanks and artillery in such large numbers not so much because the government wants it to do so, as because the country is rationally incapable of producing anything else.

The two general political models also determine the fate of the Soviet army. Indeed, War Communism permits an all-out attempt at maximum concentration or specialization of the system of production. The production made available to civil society is reduced to a minimum. The entire productive apparatus tends to fuse with the arsenals. But although War Communism makes it possible to attain short-term goals, it engenders long-term difficulties. Indeed, the production base shrinks. Coercion is such that innovation—absolutely necessary in the military domain—becomes more difficult. We know that the models for some of the most successful planes of World War II were conceived in the *sharashka** by deported engineers. A system in which research and development are placed in the hands of the prison administration is neither healthy nor stable. Enslaved and brutalized manpower is capable only of crude work. In short, the army is caught up in the general contradiction inherent in War Communism, which destroys the system through its own triumph.

On the other hand the NEP, initially unfavorable to military concerns, is beneficial to them in the long run. When all is said and done, the army draws its strength from the strength of civil society. Even though the amount siphoned off from production is proportionally smaller, the national

---

* The special scientific institutes staffed by prisoners, portrayed by Alexander Solzhenitsyn in his novel *The First Circle*.—Trans.

product increases sufficiently to enable the military's share to increase in absolute terms. Inventiveness and better workmanship can be mobilized more easily if the population has a sufficiently comfortable standard of living. This phenomenon has been evident since World War II. At his death, Stalin left an army that was bogged down in the materiel and the strategic principles that had ensured its success a decade earlier. Only with the help of the *sharashka,* deported labor, and espionage did it manage to build a number of atomic bombs. But in contrast, since 1953 the Soviet armed forces have developed prodigiously. They have perfected weapons systems that are as effective as those of the United States, and on occasion have outdistanced the Americans in inventing new systems. Starting from nothing, they have built a fleet that according to competent Sovietologists now surpasses the American fleet. Lastly, the Red Army has gained many advantages from the so-called policy of détente. But just what is détente?

By détente I mean the foreign policy of the Communist Party of the U.S.S.R., the aim of which is to apply to international society the rules determining the relationships—characteristic of the NEP—between ideological power and civil society.

As previously noted, during NEP periods the Party maintains an offensive outlook. It gives up none of its hopes of one day controlling the whole of civil society and, in the realm of foreign policy, international society. Consequently it must take advantage of the favorable conditions created by the NEP in order to strengthen itself; to maintain its unity, its discipline, and its control over the regions it administers; and to preserve the possibility of making an about-face, a new assault with conquest in mind.

I have described the new means placed at the disposal of this policy by the domestic NEP; but the "foreign NEP" also offers a series of advantages. Within the framework of System A, the Party is in a better position to profit from the ideological currents that appear simultaneously in noncommunist societies. The international communist movement is able to make use of two new circumstances in Soviet life. The decrease in the degree of repression has led progressive opinion to hope that "socialism" will assume—in fact, is on the verge of assuming, and even already *has* assumed—human proportions. That there are only one and a half million prisoners instead of twelve million is proof that "socialism and liberty are compatible." Next, civil society's undeniable increase in wealth, which is in fact caused by the contraction of the power sphere, is credited to that very same sphere. Thus the communist movement, strengthened by the improvement of its public image, can on the one hand demand additional facilities and liberties from the bourgeois states, and on the other hand impose upon the social democracies and upon Christian progressivism an esteem, a co-operation, an alliance, and even (circumstances permitting) a fusion.

Within the framework of System B, the advantages are no less clear. Détente provides an opportunity to sign a multitude of treaties—in other words, to gather in the crop most needed by the ideological regime: official recognition. Marx wrote: "Russia provides the sole example in history of an immense Empire that, even after achievements on a world scale, is still viewed as a matter for faith and not fact." Ex post facto, the formula became much more profound than in Marx's day. Indeed, since the ideological regime has only a linguistic existence, consecration of a belief becomes consecration of a "fact." Recognition of the Soviet fact by international society gives it a reality that it could not win through the most unanimous votes, the biggest parades, and the most enthusiastic adherence by domestic civil society. Just as Ulysses in Hades nourished his mother's shade with the blood of the living and caused her to assume for a moment an appearance of flesh and blood, so civil and international society make a great effort to "evoke" ideological pseudo reality and, in accordance with its demands, constantly keep it alive on this earth. For "socialism" needs these two evocators. Relying upon the approbation of civil society, it clamors for recognition by international society. Then, fortified by this recognition, it demands increased approbation from civil society.

In addition, détente possesses the same virtues as the NEP. It permits the maintenance of ideological power by civil society or, in this case, by international society. In point of fact, international society has on several occasions saved the Soviet regime in moments of crisis. I need only mention Herbert Hoover's American Relief Administration mission, which saved between five and six million peasants from starving to death during the famine of 1921, and American aid in World War II. Even during the most desperate War Communism—the War Communism of the first Five-Year Plans—the West sent the Soviet Union considerable sums of money, technology, and engineers who worked amid deported laborers. The West has never opposed the rudimentary triangular trade*—so similar to that of the eighteenth century—carried on by the Soviet government: peasants are shipped to eastern Siberia, where as deportees

---

* The classic Triangular Trade involved the exchange of rum for slaves in Africa, the exchange of slaves for sugar and molasses in the Barbados, and the exchange of sugar and molasses for rum in New England.—Trans.

they mine gold, which is then sold on the international market in order to import wheat and other merchandise whose production has become inadequate, largely owing to the initial exportation of peasants.

Détente permits a large-scale improvement upon this trade. The triangular trade is brought to perfection when the Soviet government begins to market the competitive products—weapons—that it has manufactured for the reasons discussed above. These items are sold to underdeveloped countries in exchange for stable currencies and raw materials, which are in turn sold to developed countries in exchange for equipment and technology. Above all, détente has made possible the establishment of what I shall call the "extended Witte system."

The Witte system, invented by Tsar Alexander III's famous minister of finance, consisted of getting the Allies to subsidize Russia's economic and military strength. The Allies agreed to make sizable loans that were poured into the Russian economy, the interest being paid by further loans. These Russian loans were agreed to because the Allies set great store by the Russian alliance, and because the lenders, who wanted to recover their money, deemed it in their interest to keep the Russian economy solvent. Russia's borrowing worked as a suction pump in this manner because Witte's system could be reversed at any time. It was based upon the virtual threat that the Russian government would ally itself with the Germans or declare bankruptcy. Nonetheless, Western lenders hoped that the threat would cease to be credible once Russia was sufficiently "integrated" into the world economic and political system.

The new Witte system has the following characteristics:

the item purchased is not the active military power of the U.S.S.R., but merely an appearance of good behavior within the exclusive framework of System B. Even more than in the old Witte system, the initiative lies with the states rather than with private economic agents. The latter are careful to obtain financial safeguards from their respective governments, so that the taxpayers of their countries, and not the Russian taxpayers, are the ultimate guarantors of the venture. The partners are not states allied with the U.S.S.R., but on the contrary its potential adversaries, who lack the political means to keep up their competition with the Soviets, and find it easier to purchase peace in this way. It is this shift from allies to adversaries that indicates that the Witte system has become extensive.

The Economist of November 8, 1975, credits Henry Kissinger with the following line of reasoning: "The rub of his argument is that it is desirable to sign lots of agreements with the Russians—even agreements from which Russia gets more immediate benefit than America does—because this gives future Soviet governments an investment in continued good relations with America; they won't want to lose the benefits they have won." In other words, Kissinger's thinking shows that he knows the key to the system: the threat of a political reversal. Like the lenders of old, he hopes that the long-term investment will remove the threat by integrating the U.S.S.R. into the world economic and political system.

Such reasoning would have been valid for the old Russian regime, which was not fundamentally different from those of the West; at the worst, it might have likened it to a classic tyrannical regime. But such reasoning is conspicuously weak when dealing with a communist regime.

Indeed, the guiding rule for ideological power during

an NEP period is to retain its ability to make an about-face. Ever since its birth, the Bolshevik Party has known perfectly well that, in order to remain in existence, it had to take certain precautionary measures toward civil (in this case, international) society, and it has had a long experience in doing just that. Thinking that East-West trade will "liberalize" the U.S.S.R. by the unconscious and automatic functioning of the economic "invisible hand" is to fail to understand either the Communist Party or history. The foreign NEP goes hand in hand with increased vigilance at home.

Since the Soviet State remains the sole economic initiator, there is no chance that the goods and capital seeping in from the West will turn the U.S.S.R. into a fountain of economic, much less political, pluralism. Businessmen and bankers move about like the tourists in the Soviet Union, within the hermetically sealed trips organized by Intourist. In the face of a disorganized offer, the Soviet purchasing monopoly puts the Soviet government in the best trading position. I do not know whether economists would still apply the term "market" to a situation in which there is a unilateral and total monopoly. It is probably owing to rivalries among themselves that Western businessmen speak of the Soviet "market."

The old Witte system led to a rapid development of civil society, for the influx of new capital was advantageous to a market economy. In contrast, the new Witte system leads to a strengthening of the Soviet State. Indeed, either because the imported items constitute direct supplies for the military system, or because they contribute to the support of civil society and hence permit new resources to be shifted to the military, the armed forces are the principal beneficiary of the operation. And so the foreign NEP results in an increase in the reversibility potential upon which the dynamics of the entire regime depends. Westerners think they have bought the Soviet army's abstention, in return for subsidies and a considerable increase in its potential strength. They are the ones who have made a long-term investment. They are the ones who will worry about suddenly losing the profits accruing from détente. If they begin to show what the Soviet government considers bad behavior, they may well lose all their economic investments, which is not in fact a serious matter. But above all they will find themselves in the very situation they thought détente would help them avoid—a situation now considerably worsened. They will pay for a new stay of execution by expanding the Witte system to the extent and on conditions imposed by their Soviet partner. They then will be the ones eager to sign "lots of agreements."

The Soviet government does not feel bound to international society by legal obligations. Since international society has agreed to put itself in the place of domestic civil society, the Soviet government has merely duties. Someday, at a politically opportune time, international society will have to enter the ideological sphere and become communist. It should be preparing itself. Neither Lenin, when he laid down the principles of peaceful coexistence at the beginning of NEP I, nor Brezhnev, during the current NEP, ever made any statements to the contrary. From this point of view, Soviet foreign policy denies the very idea of an international order or a concert of nations. The Soviet government assured domestic civil society that it had been given only a stay of execution, and that communization would resume once the Party was strong enough. Similarly, Soviet foreign policy held forth, with the greatest possible frankness, the promise to international society of a mere pause, to be followed by a capitulation at a time not yet determined, and for which it should be preparing at once.

Thus the Communist Party of the U.S.S.R. in good faith calls upon the capitalist world to begin, as Lenin said, to twist the rope that will hang it. It calls upon it to support and strengthen the U.S.S.R. and to refrain from criticizing "socialism," for, as in math, criticism of the U.S.S.R. is carried over to the column of the Soviet regime. By accepting détente, the West made a contract and is obliged to respect it. *Mutatis mutandis,* the very same sort of good faith was shown by the Mongol khans, who felt they had the right to demand tribute indefinitely once it had been paid by a subjugated nation. Therefore, viewed in terms of its ultimate goals, Soviet foreign policy is not that of a state just like any other.

And yet, from a different point of view, it is indeed the foreign policy of a state just like any other, and even of a state that is particularly scrupulous and respectful of contracts. In effect, having decided to allow international society (as it allowed civil society) a space, a well-defined autonomy, it decided to respect those limits to the extent that they conform to its own interest. This is a matter of political coherence. Once the Party makes the decision to set up an NEP, because the NEP is more advantageous for the Party than War Communism, it will enforce it to the utmost and will disregard the interests of its partner, who does not count ontologically. This explains why, within the framework it has itself established, the Soviet government is punctilious about its contracts, pays as promised, and keeps its word. At the end of the assigned time limit, when the agreement is about to run out, and when international society is convinced that the U.S.S.R. has returned to the fold, that society suddenly finds itself confronted once again with communism's ultimate goals, which had never been hidden from it, but which it had forgotten about, and moreover had done a great deal to make possible.

What are the goals of Soviet foreign policy? In duration and by their very nature they are, as I have said, limited only by the extent of the Universe. But, while keeping its eye on this vast horizon, the Soviet Communist Party establishes goals for itself that are different within the framework of an NEP policy from those established during War Communism. During the NEP (or détente) the goals are indefinite in extent but limited in intensity.

They are indefinite in extent because the whole of international society, which has assumed an NEP position, is the concern of the Soviet government. Under such circumstances the government puts the talent and means at its disposal in the service of its diplomacy. Indeed, its political activism is no longer satisfied by domestic activities. At home it must be satisfied with administering its acquisitions, so that domestic policy during an NEP period is not very interesting. But on the other hand, beyond its borders there are stimulating and exciting games to play. The triangular trade and the new Witte system are applicable to the entire world. The whole universe must contribute to the prosperity of the Soviet State and the international communist movement. Systems A and B are fully utilized within a policy that becomes world-wide by its own momentum, and that cannot dissociate itself from any region of the globe. Strengthening the Soviet State and preparing the conditions necessary for the expansion of world communism are two permanent tasks that do not recognize geographical limits.

But these tasks do recognize *limits in intensity,* which are the limits of the NEP itself. As far as domestic policy is concerned, the NEP's rule is to refrain, for the time being, from killing the goose that lays the golden egg. The same rule applies to foreign policy. To ask whether détente implies that the U.S.S.R. has given up "exporting revolution" is to ask a deceptive question. It has "given it up" temporarily because it is making preparations to do successfully just that, and it needs a delay to be certain of ultimate success. As long as détente is advantageous to the strength of the Soviet State and the international communist movement, why cut it short? Using the terminology of traditional diplomacy, we can say that as a general rule—though local circumstances can predispose otherwise—NEP aims to influence rather than to dominate directly. It confines both international and civil society within fences, where they live under surveillance, until the Party can regroup its forces and put them under its direct control.

Such is détente as we have been living it since the first trips that Malenkov and his companion Bulganin made in 1954 to announce it to the West. We should now ask the reasons that can lead to the abandonment of so advantageous a policy, and what foreign policy corresponds to what, at home, would be a return to War Communism.

It would be fruitless to search for these reasons in the international system. The U.S.S.R. paid an extraordinarily low price to obtain subsidies from its adversaries, whose death it still kept promising. In most instances the Soviets had only to ask—indeed, to accept the offers that came. Had it not been for certain individuals, détente might have been even more extensive, might have moved on to co-operation and even become collaboration in the complete sense that Pierre Laval gave the word in 1942. According to Gustav Flaubert, the banker Dambreuse was so terrified by the horrors of the Revolution of 1848 that he "would have paid in order to sell himself," that is, to turn traitor. Capitalism at times is gutless!

The reasons are to be sought in the domestic sphere. At home, détente aggravates the consequences of the NEP. Its indirect influence is in the long run tangible. By allowing noncommunist societies to live as they see fit, and by formally declaring peaceful coexistence, détente feeds the hopes of domestic civil society. Civil society has never had the benefit of any solemn promises. Nor does it enjoy a comparable autonomy. It is at the very most tolerated, and none of the repressive laws that weigh upon it have been abolished, but merely suspended or laxly enforced. Peasants, workers, intellectuals, nations, and believers look with hope beyond the frontiers of communist domination. Instinctively they form a common cause with the outside world, which they imagine to be more perfect than it is, embellishing it with their dreams and their desires. For them, the outside is utopia come true. This is what makes the outside dangerous. Taught by experience, the Soviet peoples are not counting upon active aid from the West; it is enough that the West exists. Subject to propaganda that tries to make them believe in the solidity of ideological pseudo reality, they contrast the impossible utopia of communism with the utopia-come-true of the outside world, the natural goal of their spontaneous development. It is the same with the outside world as with the personal language: merely by existing, the outside world volatilizes the false ideology. That is why, détente or not, travel is still forbidden.

Moreover, détente can become an obstacle to the adoption of a new political about-face toward War Communism.

This is undoubtedly more true on the periphery of the Empire than at its center. The European buffer zone of the U.S.S.R. includes at least two states—Hungary and Poland—where the NEP assumed extreme forms, far beyond anything ever encountered in the Soviet Republic. In Poland, civil society has swelled to such proportions that at times the communist apparatus is imperceptible. The regime no longer is visible save in the general poverty, the usual inefficiency, the control of public speech and official texts, and the police. That is not enough. Who knows but that the NEP has reached a point of no return beyond which Polish communism, which already survives only because of Soviet occupation, will need a massive dose of "fraternal help" and "proletarian internationalism" to reconquer the country. Poland lives in this fear. As for Czechoslovakia, there drastic emergency measures had to be taken to reimpose War Communism. Despite the West's good will, this was, as our newspapers and statesmen admit, "a blow to détente." Could Poland and Hungary be put down in the same fashion without temporarily ending détente?

Destroying civil society, extending absolute control over it, and forcing its return to utopia—such goals will oblige the Communist Party to mobilize all its forces for domestic tasks. But before attempting such a risky political venture, its has to be on firm footing internationally. It has recently gone through that sort of situation: the period known as the Cold War, which corresponds to War Communism III during the postwar years. What was the Cold War like?

From a distance, it seems that on the Soviet side it was basically a policy aimed at the economy. The Red Army had conquered a certain number of European countries, and System A had immediately set up communist institutions there. Soviet diplomacy, at minimal cost and with minimal risk, made sure that Sovietization would be carried out calmly within the conquered zone. Beyond the frontiers of that zone, foreign policy showed little activity. It had few concrete means at its disposal. Although it assured the safety of its capital investments in Europe—that is, the safety of the Communist Parties of France, Italy, and a few other countries—it gave up actively influencing the zones not under its direct control. The West, which had been watching the Sovietization of the East with some degree of horror, and which saw most resources (as always, during War Communism) going to the army, thought that the Soviets posed a threat. Within itself, the West found the will to take the necessary countermeasures. The U.S.S.R.'s few foreign adventures—the Berlin blockade and the Korean War—seem to have been the fruit of Stalin's tyrannical and irresponsible caprice, and not the decision of the Party, which later disavowed them.

If, therefore, the ideal model of the Cold War is defined by contrasting it with the ideal model of détente, we can say that fundamentally its goals are *indefinite in intensity* but *limited in extent*. Indefinite in intensity because the external zones—which are under the direct power of the Communist Party—are treated like domestic society: that is, they are supposed to fit into the molds foreseen by ideology. This is what happened to the People's Republics after World War II. It is a matter of persuading society that no model exists other than the one it is being urged to conform to. The Cold War policy accentuates the characteristic uniformity by which the logocratic regime can be recognized. From Vietnam to Weimar, from Havana to Yemen, one finds the same leader, the same language, the same newspapers, the same forms of social behavior. The mimesis reaches all the way to the international communist movement. The Cold War was the era when the French Communist Party took pride in imitating the Bolshevik Party in everything: mannerisms, the life style of the leaders, and even the purge trial, which was an exact copy of the trials of Rajk and Slansky,* except that instead of disappearing into the shadows of death, the guilty ones disappeared into the outer shadows of exclusion from the Party. The Party was concerned above all with its purity, its integrity, the precision of its contours.

By contrast, the extension of this policy is limited geographically. It deliberately remains within the boundaries of the zone under its direct control. Not that the Party has given up world empire; but at this juncture, its vision has changed from centrifugal to centripetal. The Manichaeism has altered its form. In détente, socialism and capitalism confront each other and are intimately enmeshed in a cosmic battle. But now the frontiers become uncrossable moats, iron curtains; *We* and *They* are separated, not to mingle. The uncontrolled zones are abandoned to the enemy, and it is just as well if the enemy assumes hideous forms—"fascism" and "imperialism"—that can be denounced immediately. The Cold War attempts to apply to international society the rules that are valid for civil society. It wraps international society in the dilemma of absolute enmity or subjection. Détente, like the NEP, strives for exploitation, whereas the Cold War, like War Communism, seeks violent transformation whenever possible. Again, in the terms used by traditional diplomacy—though here, too, circumstances

---

* Laszlo Rajk, a leading Hungarian communist, was tried on questionable charges and executed in October 1949. Rudolf Slansky, a high-ranking Czech communist, was similarly tried and executed in November 1952.—Trans.

can predispose differently—the Cold War seeks direct local domination rather than world influence. Serving the inner-oriented policy of War Communism, it strives for stability.

Détente is diplomacy based upon movement. The Cold War is diplomacy based upon immobility. The best illustration is the figure of Mr. Nyet, on stage during the good old days at the United Nations. But the Cold War can assume an impressive and much more disturbing appearance than détente. In undecided zones it strives to seize power, without excessive regard for soothing public opinion. It makes little difference whether the coup at Prague results in the ousting of communist ministers in Paris or Rome. The important thing is to add up gains and losses, to reach a clean-cut division, a stable situation that lets one tend to the engrossing task of "constructing socialism."

War and Peace

In history, as elsewhere, facts can be grasped and understood only through a comprehensive theoretical construction. By using the couples of War Communism and NEP, and Cold War and détente, I have sketched out a framework within which a maximum number of political phenomena become intelligible. In order to prove or disprove the theory, I have searched history, and in so doing have excluded nuances and specific cases. NEP and War Communism, détente and Cold War, are political models superimposed upon one another like tracing paper. Their counterparts existed in the pre-1917 Bolshevik Party, which used the criterion of reversibility to determine its unitarian or sectarian tactics.

NEP and détente, War Communism and Cold War, have clear affinities as pairs; but as political models they can be separated and applied locally, out of phase, as an exception to the general pattern. Thus, the Sovietization of Cuba took advantage of a favorable local situation, though it also was a splinter in détente. Despite the Cuban episode, however, détente kept progressing elsewhere, and the communist movement did not have to relax its domination of the island. On the other hand, just after World War II—through a whim of Stalin's, it seems—a very pure and stable form of détente was established with Finland.

But this schema is no help at all for predicting the future. It does not even permit us to say with any certainty whether the Soviet government will become deeply committed to a new about-face, or whether it will continue—as it has been doing since 1964—to tack back and forth between the two models described, without making, or perhaps being able to make, a clear decision. The validity of the two models will not be brought into doubt, even if they no longer correspond to the pure types they represented in the past. Only retrospectively can we judge whether, since 1964, the Soviet government has contented itself by design with keeping the NEP within acceptable limits—with the help of a few pokes in the ribs that resemble abortive about-faces toward War Communism—or whether War Communism is their conscious aim.

How will it all come out? History is a continual surprise. The ideology propounds an impersonal and transparent vision of history. But history itself is, on the contrary, personal and mysterious. No theory will ever make us masters of fate, but at least it can help us understand ourselves at present. From the infinitely complex game of international politics, where no leading actor has a synoptic vision (and this particular author least of all), a number of questions arise; it is not certain that these questions have been properly stated, but they haunt chancelleries and the editorial offices of newspapers. If he asks my opinion, I can neither ignore the questions of the man in the street nor hide behind my "learning." Let us try to answer, with complete uncertainty, a few of these frank questions.

.　.　.

Does Brezhnev sincerely want détente? To me, the answer seems to be, "Yes, of course." Détente is not a concession that the Communist Party of the U.S.S.R. makes to its adversaries; it is a deliberate policy that the Party is trying to impose upon those adversaries. In addition, even when the Party shifts, with equal determination, to the other model of foreign policy, it does not give up détente, or at any rate the benefits of détente. If it cannot reap them across the entire surface of this planet, it will strive to harvest them locally. Confronted with the Nazi threat in the 1930s, Stalin knew how, in the midst of War Communism, to play the détente game with democratic countries; yet at the same time he was endeavoring to Sovietize the Spanish Republic as completely as possible. He also knew how, after the Nazi-Soviet Pact of 1939, to conduct a remarkably pure policy of détente with Hitler. This was perhaps the only case of bilateral détente, in which each of the two partners got the other to provide support, while still consciously planning to destroy that other partner at a later date. Détente, like the NEP, is asymmetrical. To be reciprocal, it must be used by two ideological states each upon the other. Détente or cold war could very well determine the relationships between the various communist states.

Even after the clearest signs of "hardening" (as they call it) have appeared, we must wait until Brezhnev, with increased vigor, accuses the West of betraying détente. Here he will once again be in the right, if international society stops behaving as it ought to during a period of détente, and balks at submitting to the "laws of history."

Some Western experts—among them Harrison Salisbury —have said repeatedly that a Sino-Soviet war is imminent.

In his letter to the Soviet leaders Solzhenitsyn thinks it highly probable, almost inevitable. In the People's Republics of Eastern Europe there is a muffled hope for it. I do not know the military plans of the Red Army, but cannot help having the greatest doubts.

I do not think that China is the dynamic power whose pressure Solzhenitsyn fears. It is plausible that the Communist Revolution has capsized the illustrious Chinese nation, just as earlier it capsized the very dynamic Russian Empire. When you think of Japan's development since the war, and the prosperity of Taiwan, Hong Kong, and Singapore, you find yourself imagining how China might have developed with an entire continent at its disposal, and what pressure it could have exerted upon the southern flank of a sparsely populated Siberia and a colonized Turkestan. Today that frontier separates two systems of concentration camps. The labor camps of Magadan and Kolyma hold little attraction for the boarders in the "May Seventh schools," the "Northern Communes," and other euphemisms with which the Chinese adorn the harsh reality of their concentration camps. The same is true on the Russian side of the border. "The time since 1949," writes Solzhenitsyn, "has evidently not been enough for the [Chinese] population to lose its high degree of fundamental industriousness (which is higher than ours is today)."* Who knows? One does not with impunity mobilize an industrious people to do absurd tasks. One does not with impunity force a polite, skeptical, and shrewd people to chant in chorus the thoughts of Chairman Mao. For twenty-five years China has seemed entangled in an abortive War Communism that appears unable to take root completely, that miscarries before bear-

* Solzhenitsyn, *Letter*, pp. 13–14.

ing its full fruit. I do not picture China hatching a plan for military aggression against its great neighbor.

And the U.S.S.R.? Will it go to war in order to prove, as Solzhenitsyn has also said, that "the sacred truth is written on page 533 of Lenin and not on page 335"?*

It would be very serious for all these ideological regimes if pluralism and free speech were reborn somewhere within their world-wide Empire. Unlike all revolutions in the past, the communist revolutions have until now not been followed by a restoration. By "restoration" I mean the abandonment of utopian goals, and the end of the schism between ordinary reality and ideological reality. The great English Revolution of the 1640s and the French Revolution experienced restorations. The Nazi revolution had one forced upon it. But in Hungary, in Czechoslovakia, a restoration was smothered in the cradle. For each of the peoples living under "socialism," this teaches the important, heartbreaking lesson that history never turns backward, and that their future is committed for eternity to the impossible task of making utopia tangible. The regime requires that the dead word's monopoly not be contested. It matters little whether this word is found on page 533 or on page 335, since it is not supposed to be believed, but, rather, to do away with the living word. In Hungary, in Czechoslovakia, the regime was perfectly correct in crushing the pluralistic decomposition of the communist parties and in normalizing public utterance: the risk of contagion would have been too great. But in China the monopoly has not been questioned. On the contrary, the destruction of culture, language, and morals seems even more complete than in the U.S.S.R. China—joined by Rumania—certainly is hampering the interna-

* *Ibid.,* p. 17.

tional activities of the Soviet regime. Yet it does not constitute a mortal threat to that regime. In this sense the China question remains an internal problem for the international communist movement; it is not urgent.

But China is also a state whose independence is especially difficult to overcome, because Leninist ideology has formed a close alliance there with nationalism. It therefore poses a foreign-policy problem applicable to both System A and System B. We know that the Soviet Party is trying to gain supporters and accomplices within the Chinese Party. We also know that a sizable part of the Soviet army is stationed along the Chinese frontier. The U.S.S.R. will do its utmost, of course, to weaken the People's Republic of China. One would think that it would try to nip China's atomic strength in the bud. But it is not doing so.

There are many reasons for the U.S.S.R.'s caution or failure to act, but I should like to emphasize that a policy toward China could not develop within the political framework either of a détente or of a Cold War. Détente is only advantageous if the society that agrees to it generates wealth, and if that wealth can be tapped by the Soviet system. The Chinese regime's greatest achievement, during good years, has been to fill the rice bowls of its subjects while still maintaining its formidable army. China has no wheat surplus, no gold or bank-note reserves. Besides, how could the Soviet Party think of applying War Communism to Chinese society? China is not East Germany, either in past history or in size. Its own Party is inadequate to the task. In short, according to the two models I have proposed, China can be neither exploited nor transformed. So doesn't that make a waiting policy advisable?

The specter of the Chinese danger is, of course, just as useful to Soviet domestic policy as the Russian danger is to

Chinese domestic policy. It is not impossible that war would break out for reasons whose rationality I do not perceive. But I do not see how it could be justifiable in strategic terms. A victory by either side would not permanently settle the great cosmic confrontation between communism and capitalism. It would be a dangerous war, a war impossible to win, a war waged in an impoverished country, a war that would exhaust both parties. Of all the battlefields that could be chosen for the great confrontation, this would be the worst choice of all.

All the reasons that deflect the spearhead of Soviet foreign policy from China turn it upon Europe. Strategically, Europe is decisive. If isolated from the United States, it can be conquered almost without a fight. Sometimes we hear the objection that the U.S.S.R., already having enough trouble with its own half of Europe, would have even more if it controlled the other half, too. The argument can be turned around: it would be easier to defend its buffer zone if the latter were no longer a buffer zone. Just as Austria-Hungary hoped to solve the problem of the Slavs in the south by subduing the Serbian bastion in 1914, so the U.S.S.R. would find it easier to govern Eastern Europe by adding Western Europe to its orbit.

Europe is the best terrain in which to apply a policy of détente. It is wealthy. It is divided. The communist movement's greatest success, within System A, has been to perpetuate this division. The division by now is so ingrained that the methods of System B suffice to keep it going. In France official spokesmen even came forward and declared that the unification of Europe was impossible, and that it was undesirable to form an integrated European defense, since the "Soviet government does not want it." A substantial but insufficient defense structure, which could not oppose an about-face—that is in effect what civil society is allowed under the NEP, and what international society is allowed under détente. France's ministers were showing that they knew the rules of the game. One has the right not to be communist, but not the right to be anticommunist; the right to be "capitalist," but not anti-Soviet. France has nothing but friends; its army has no specified enemy.

But Europe is a terrain where the Cold War policy would also bear good fruit. As I have said, the Cold War aims to divide, to transform on the local scale, to make a precise reckoning of gains and losses. Circumstances may favor a new division that will put zones disregarded since 1945 within the sphere of active communization. After all, there are more communists in the smallest township of Western Europe than in all Eastern Europe, although most of them can be accused of naiveté. Once the means of expression were seized, the market suppressed, social classes broken up, intermediary bodies destroyed, and frontiers closed— so that each people, confined within its corral, could not communicate with its neighbor—nothing would upset things for a long time to come. The Sovietization of Eastern Europe has kept the communist movement busy for ten years. What a rich field of activity Western Europe would be! How invigorating to get one's second wind!

The most perspicacious observers were surprised that the U.S.S.R. encountered so few difficulties in getting the European states to meet at Helsinki, when it seems to have serious trouble bringing together the communist parties of those very same countries. Why does System B—an inter-state system, and therefore by nature disputatious—in this instance function more flexibly than System A, which works through the international communist movement? Until now, the European Communist Parties seem to have agreed upon an unusually modest program, whose style is more appropriate to conversations among states than to debates among Communist Parties.

At Helsinki the Western states were asked, with unusual solemnity, once again to acquiesce in détente. They did, while nonetheless taking a few precautions to make sure that verbal equivocation would persist, and that people would not know whether the word had the precise meaning the U.S.S.R. gives it, or its meaning in ordinary speech. They managed to have it mean both things at once. The U.S.S.R. voiced its interpretation loud and clear, while the West was content to keep its interpretation more or less vague. But there was another aspect to Helsinki: drawing a sharp and impassable line around those zones of Europe already Sovietized. This forceful reminder of the limits that international society must not cross during a regime of détente may have been a way of indicating that détente was coming to an end, and of announcing an impending about-face. The formula "What is ours is ours, what is yours is negotiable" can apply to détente as well as to the Cold War, depending on whether "ours" or "negotiable" is emphasized; on what is about to be done to "ours"; and on the remoteness or proximity of the expiration date of the "negotiation."

The signals were too subtle for the Western states to understand. Did they even know the true meaning of détente? Did they know where they were heading? If so, wouldn't it be better to sign another treaty in order to prolong détente? So that tomorrow will be like yesterday.

On the other hand, the Communist Parties of Europe must be congratulated for having interpreted these signals perfectly. If, as seems plausible, they know that the Communist Party of the U.S.S.R. is leaning toward an about-face, that it is thinking of going back to War Communism, that as a result it is promoting a new Cold War, then we can understand why they are taking divergent paths according to their own individual interests.

The goal of the Communist Parties of Europe is to gain power, and not—as in the U.S.S.R.—to keep it. Only after taking power can they choose between the policies of War Communism and the NEP. The European Communist Parties are by nature unfamiliar with such a choice. Their strategies, though structurally similar, belong to an older layer of Leninism in which sectarianism and opportunism, leftism and liquidationism, and so forth, are set up in opposition to one another within a totally different context.

Administering utopia is one thing, preparing its arrival is another. The individual rhythm of each of the Communist Parties does not coincide with the rhythm of the Soviet Communist Party. Of course they are aware that they belong to the same international communist movement. They know how important the existence of the Soviet State is to them, and how necessary it is to maintain unity within the movement. Rationally, out of political cohesion, they obey "proletarian internationalism." Annie Kriegel correctly noted that the Western communists follow Moscow's party line because they are Bolsheviks, not because Moscow compels them by remote control. They are dependent, though totally independent. However, this difference in rhythm is a source of tension. In order to help the sister parties resolve these tensions, the Soviet Party maintains a semisecret apparatus within their midst, whose existence they tolerate. Normally these tensions are more acute when Moscow's about-face from one policy to another forces one of the sister parties to give up temporarily a policy it has adopted while pursuing the inalterable goal of gaining power just as it is beginning to bear fruit.

If a new Cold War once again divides Europe into an expanded Bolshevized zone and a more limited (if I dare use the word) "free" zone, it is to be expected that a Party will balk at finding itself in the zone being sacrificed. How hard it will be, far from those in power, to face isolation, to defend the U.S.S.R. to everyone and against everything, as was necessary after the Nazi-Soviet Pact of 1939 or the Berlin blockade, and, once the front line has shifted, to find oneself in the same situation in which civil society was confined under the NEP!

Circumstances and party policy have now put the Communist Parties on the brink of power in France and Italy. As Raymond Aron has noted, for the first time they can imagine conquering the state through society, and not, as had been the rule up to now, society through the state. The differences between the two Parties over this new party line can perhaps be explained by a difference in the way they have assessed their chances of assuming power within a climate of détente or Cold War. In addition, the Italian Communist Party is suspect for another reason: it has gone too far in its policy of alliances, and consequently has lost its ability to make a political about-face; it has thus fallen into opportunism, which sooner or later leads to a change in the very nature of the Party, to a social democratization. Far be it from me to venture an opinion. Considering that culture, the means of expression, is under even greater ideological control in Italy than in France, I wonder whether the suspicion is well founded. Détente strengthens the civil society surrounding the Communist Party of the U.S.S.R. It also strengthens it around the European Communist Parties. The French Communist Party has stood up to this erosion very well. It is not certain that the Italian Communist Party, which is very involved with civil society, has equaled its French counterpart on this score. A return to the Cold War would help the international communist movement remain true to itself.

The prospect of a division accounts quite well for the differences between the Portuguese and the Spanish Communist Parties. As if on military maneuvers, following the strict Bolshevik *Kriegspiel,* Alvaro Cunhal's Party courageously attacked those in power, in one of the most faithfully executed classroom exercises ever witnessed in the scenario of the October Revolution. But Santiago Carillo has a much more dangerous question of succession to manipulate. His Party also is suspected of opportunism. It is tempting to continue this analysis, but I might lose all touch with reality. Time will tell.

The Yom Kippur War can serve as an example of the local profits that the U.S.S.R. allows itself to amass, within the framework of détente, whenever the occasion arises. To make certain of the Arab alliance, to humble Israel, weaken Europe's southern flank, and use oil as blackmail— all were juicy prospects. The collapse of the Zionist project would discourage Soviet Jews and, along with them, the nationalities seeking emancipation. So it was worth the trouble to arm and train the Arabs, and to risk a fight. Victory was not necessary. The Soviet plan merely required that Israel not win a crushing victory over the Arabs. Indeed, Israel's mere presence assured the U.S.S.R. of the Arabs' loyalty or dependence. In the event of an inconclusive victory, Israel would be forced to negotiate from a position of weakness. Then the U.S.S.R. could step in as mediator and make the most of its "moderation." It would pocket the political benefits of the operation and moreover, by accepting the survival of a weakened Israel, not endanger détente. On the contrary, it could impose détente with increased vigor. However, the Yom Kippur War did not produce the hoped-for results, owing to Israel's military performance and America's energetic response. Since 1973 the picture has changed.

The hypothesis of a trend toward division seems to find as much confirmation in the Middle East as in Europe. Here too we find a territory hanging in the balance: Lebanon. The U.S.S.R.'s formal recognition of Israel, which was very advantageous as long as it applied the general scheme of détente to the Middle East, loses its importance within the context of a Cold War. It can hinder the clear demarcation between friends and enemies, controlled zones and other zones.

The United Nations resolution of November 1975, denouncing Zionism as a form of racism, therefore seems to me to have been instigated by the U.S.S.R. Indeed, racism is not part of the vocabulary of the Arab world. It belongs to the vocabulary of Nazism and anti-Nazism. Until this U.N. resolution, the word had a relatively specific meaning, since it was applied to races that really existed, although in a totally different manner from the pseudo biology of racism. Applying the word to Zionism, which is based upon the notion of a people and categorically repudiates the notion of race, makes the concept of racism part of radical untruth. Henceforth "racism," like "imperialism" and "fascism," belongs to that group of imprecise notions that can be applied to anyone and anything, according to the immediate interest of ideological power, in which respect Bolshevism has always been superior to Nazi ideology. The remnants of détente will be used to make international society accept this vocabulary. In addition, at home it will be easy to impose, on those Jews who wish to emigrate, the severe punishments that Soviet law has stipulated for persons demonstrating racism and anti-Semitism.

But here I must halt this brief survey of international current events, for I want to discuss yet another continuing theme in the foreign policy of the Communist Party of the U.S.S.R.

The inordinate mushrooming of the Soviet armed forces seems to put the world in danger of war. In 1939 Germany went to war seriously unprepared, in a risky strategic situation, and having given no thought to war on a world-wide scale. On all these points the Red Army seems in a better position. If it becomes convinced, rightly or wrongly, that it can advantageously carry on the "same policy" by means of war, and not risk mutual annihilation, the temptation will be greater in the future than in the days when the army barely maintained a precarious equivalence with its principal adversary.

Anything can happen. However, I want to stress that, in the ideological sphere, resorting to war is a notion that is out of bounds. The notion of détente is part of the Soviet vocabulary, where it is translated, with more conceptual precision, as *relaxation of tension*. But not the notion of the Cold War. For convenience I have employed that expression, which originated in the West, to designate one of the two models of Soviet foreign policy, although throughout this analysis I have put myself in the place of the Communist Party of the U.S.S.R., and have borrowed its vocabulary. If you were to look at some Soviet texts from the period of the Cold War—in its historical sense,

1945–1953—you would find another name: the *defense of peace*. Throughout its history, Soviet foreign policy has oscillated between the *defense of peace* and the *relaxation of tension*.

If you place yourself within the ideology, these names seem perfectly justified. Just as there is no true liberty in a country such as France, since the communists are not fully in power, so likewise there is no stable peace in the world, since communism must share the terrain and struggle unremittingly to impose its existence—even where it is already the master—in the face of an elusive enemy, an enemy from the outside, called imperialism. So the construction of socialism is inseparable from the defense of peace. Along the borders of Eastern Europe, which was undergoing Sovietization, Soviet troops patrolled for peace. The defense of peace is active, and on occasion takes the offensive. When the Warsaw Pact troops invaded Czechoslovakia and put in an appearance for proletarian internationalism, they also were defending peace, as Gustáv Husák* stated publicly. During détente the construction of socialism is postponed, or at least slowed down. The relaxation of tension therefore becomes possible. But when construction resumes and there is what journalists call a "hardening," a "stiffening," then peace must be defended.

It is also possible to put yourself outside the ideological sphere and learn the same lesson. Raymond Aron is fond of emphasizing that, according to Clausewitz, the one who wages war is not the one who invades his neighbor at the head of an army. If the neighbor bows before the violence, the violence does not develop into a war. The one who begins a war honorably is the one who uses his weapons in self-defense. The U.S.S.R. did not wage war against Czecho-

---

* President of the Republic of Czechoslovakia.

slovakia, because Czechoslovakia had not started a war against the U.S.S.R.

Therefore nothing prevents Western Europe from understanding where its true well-being is. The Soviet army does not exist to coerce, but to persuade. Its role is pedagogical. It conveys the laws of history, and is the *ultima ratio* of the ideology. The decision to make war does not belong essentially to the Soviet government, which will always conceive of itself as bound by its continuing policy of peace. It is our decision. The Red Army's entry into Western Europe, if that should one day occur, will never be considered an act of war by the Soviet government. That government doubtlessly would act in such a manner that we ourselves would not view it as aggression, but as protection or liberation, and so would welcome it with flowers.

The True Lie and the False Lie

What now? Should I turn the coin over and talk about the United States and its allies or—as they say so inaccurately—about the West? This is a very different subject, one that does not fit into this little book. It is a more difficult subject, for the West cannot be analyzed with models as simple as those regulating Soviet policy. Our world is concrete, involved, complicated, as varied as nature. Not having been born of a theory, it does not lend itself to theorization. The Soviet world defies comprehension because of its abstractness, yet because of that same abstractness, it is simple.

Let us simplify the problem. Let us eliminate the West's domestic policy. Let us refrain from any discussion of the "crisis in the West." In foreign policy, let us handle only our relations with the Soviet government. Let us ask this one basic question: What is our intellectual difficulty in understanding the Soviet government's foreign policy? After all, that foreign policy is not at all esoteric. I have limited myself to presenting a system of thought that can be found in its entirety in Lenin's works. These are made available at low cost in every language by the very government whose intentions have provoked so many questions over the past sixty years. In the final analysis, what do the Soviets want?

They are trying very hard to tell us. Why do our most sophisticated Sovietologists keep endlessly asking one another what takes the place of thoughts in the heads of diplomats whose appearance evokes neither the guile of the Renaissance Venetians nor the subtlety of their Florentine contemporaries? Gromyko, who has alternately been administering the Cold War and détente for twenty-five years, has nothing of a Talleyrand about him. Why, when confronted by those dead-pan faces and those labored civilities that they themselves would never use, do our diplomats sometimes have the vague feeling of having been duped?

One remark will bring us closer to the answer. Since Germany's surrender, Western policy has set up for itself objectives that coincide miraculously with those of Soviet policy. During the Cold War John Foster Dulles's policy was summed up by the word "containment." To be sure, although War Communism is aimed at division, this division is forced upon it by circumstances. It was not of their own free will that the Soviet leaders halted their Sovietization at the Elbe River. If they had encountered merely a vacuum there, Sovietization would have progressed beyond the river. It was halted by American strength, and at that point preferred gains in depth to superficial ones. From then on, it is hard to see what policy would have been more agreeable to the U.S.S.R. than one establishing a defensive cordon around the "peacekeeper." The frontier separating the subjugated zone from the relinquished zone simply became more consolidated, which was indeed one of the goals of Soviet policy.

The West's reply to détente was even more symmetrical. *Containment* can be considered an approximate equivalent of *defense of peace*. But from the outset, the *relaxation of tension* seemed a goal to be attained in common. The same word, the same expression, became a slogan shared by great powers which, however, were each building up arms to use against the other. It was just as if the West had spontaneously begun to play the role its Soviet partner had created for it, without first insisting upon a political advantage in exchange for its abstention from defending peace, or its collaboration in relaxing tension—as if it had adopted the very same goals, and would be satisfied once it had attained them. The West is arming in order to avoid the consequences of Soviet foreign policy, but it has never tried to dispute the basic principle of that foreign policy. A "rollback" was never seriously considered, no more than the possibility of rejecting détente and locking the U.S.S.R. up in its ghetto the instant it showed signs of wanting to leave it.

I see only one continuing and mutual theme in this policy adopted by the Western powers: they want the U.S.S.R. to enter into the concert of powers. They are treating the U.S.S.R. as if it were just like any other state, in the hope that it will finally behave that way, will actually be what they want it to be. In short, their action is pedagogical. During a period of defense of peace, they defend peace by clearly noting the limits that must not be crossed, for fear of war. During a period of détente, they follow the etiquette book that governs relations among states that have decided to coexist, so that their partner will gradually learn to follow these rules, too. It is a question of establishing a common language in which peace and war have a common meaning.

Western powers have at their disposal a test to gauge the intentions of Soviet foreign policy: Is it giving up "exporting the Revolution"? The day when System A is dismantled once and for all, and when Soviet policy uses only the means of System B, the U.S.S.R. will have gained international respectability.

In this regard the test has been negative. The Comintern had scarcely been dissolved, when the Cominform assumed its role. Dissolved in turn, the Cominform's functions are now being carried on by the Central Committee's commission in charge of relations with the sister Parties. At one point the French government proved to be a stickler about the principle of national independence, and boasted about its perfect agreement with the Soviet government on this point. Yet it did not take offense when the selection of the general secretary of the largest political party in France was made in consultation with a specialized commission of the Soviet government, to which this general secretary very openly submitted a report several times a year.

To give up exporting the Revolution is something the Soviet government could not do, even if it wanted to. That would mean giving up ideology, and consequently giving up power. Whether it is believed, as it still largely is within the communist movement of Western Europe, or whether it merely receives lip service, as in the Soviet Empire, the ideology has the same form, the same content. And it strives for universality. It was no weak ambition that caused the earliest communists to coalesce around Lenin. They wanted to create a new heaven and a new earth, to rebuild the social and the natural world, to make the old world give birth to a new world as the doctrine promised. Their vision of the universe was not restricted by any previously determined limits. It was a vision with a focus. At the center of things it placed an absolute knowledge that gradually reorganized about itself the whole spectrum of learning, even

Lysenko's genetics and Marr's linguistics. One ambition, one divine vision. This, and this alone, is the basis of the legitimacy of communist power. If that power were to give up trying to dominate the Universe, it would lose its right to dominate the least little township. It is penned up within an all-or-nothing situation that condemns it to be nothing if it does not strive to be everything. The sister Parties are united with one another in their solidarity with the U.S.S.R. It is just as true the other way around.

But this still is not the key to the enigma. The paradox, the disconcerting and fallacious reasoning, has a different cause. For utopia cannot be attained simply because utopia has gained power. Here is a divergence that sixty years of effort have not been able to eliminate, a divergence between what the U.S.S.R. ought to be in order to prove the doctrine, and what it is. If the utopia had been a moral one, the divergence between the desired and the achieved would be bearable, and communism would have been an "ideal" toward which it was possible to strive without claiming to attain that ideal. "Therefore sanctify yourselves, and ye shall be holy; for I am holy," God says to his people (Leviticus 11:44). They try, knowing that they cannot succeed. But this utopia was a scientific one. It is natural that pseudo nature should be born of nature, and pseudo reality of reality. But pseudo reality was not born. It has not even begun to be born. The Russian Empire was subjugated, churned up a thousand times over, kneaded, and poured into the ideological mold, but its matter refused to retain that shape. Between the U.S.S.R. of the honest reporting and the U.S.S.R. of the newspapers, official magazines, and vacuum-packed tourists, a gap developed—the same absolute, unclosable gap that has existed since the very first day The ideology remained a ghost in search of a body. Its incarnation did not occur. Socialism remained —if I may use a theological term—*docetic*.* The construction of socialism amounted to the construction of a fiction.

Alas, Russia traditionally had a gift for playing this role. "Russia deceives and lies," wrote Jules Michelet in his *Légendes démocratiques du Nord*. "It is a phantasmagoria, a mirage, it is the empire of illusion . . . a crescendo of lies, false pretenses, and illusions."

Nearly a century later, in 1938, and speaking from the weight of experience, Boris Souvarine wrote:

The U.S.S.R. is the country of the lie, the absolute lie, the integral lie. Stalin and his subjects are always lying, at every moment, under every circumstance, and by dint of lying they no longer even realize that they are lying. Where everything lies, nothing lies. The U.S.S.R. is nothing but a lie based on fact. In the four words those initials stand for, there are no fewer than four lies. The Constitution contains several lies per article. The lie is the natural element of the pseudo-Soviet society. Stalin, according to the fundamental law, does not exist: a lie. The Politburo, according to official documents, never existed: a lie. The Party, the elite of the population: a lie. The rights of the people, democracy, freedoms: lies. The Five-Year Plans, statistics, results, accomplishments: lies. . . . Assemblies, congresses: theater, stage production. Dictatorship of the proletariat: an immense fraud. The spontaneity of the masses: meticulous organization. Right, left: a lie and another lie. Stakhanov:† a liar. Stakhanovism: a lie. The merry life: a

* In the early Church, Docetism was a tendency (rather than a formulated and unified doctrine) that considered the humanity and sufferings of the earthly Christ as apparent rather than real.—Trans.
† In the mid-1930s Stakhanov, an overzealous worker, tried to increase the efficiency of factory workers by means of a quota system. This system was called stakhanovism.—Trans.

mournful farce. The new Soviet man: an old gorilla. Culture: nonculture. An inspired leader: an obtuse tyrant. Socialism: a shameless lie.

I agree with his judgment on all but one point: the lie is not a *true* lie.

Forty years have passed since Souvarine made this statement. Millions of Russians have come into the world, grown old, died. The fields have turned green many times, have changed their shapes. Immense cities, colossal factories have been built, have become dilapidated. All of this has been born, grown to maturity, and passed on to senility. One thing has eluded the life cycle: socialism. It existed as a theory in Lenin's mind. Lenin assumed power on November 7, 1917, but socialism remained a theory. Power was maintained, reality evolved, but socialism kept the purity, the incorruptibility of nonexistence. So how was communist power to proceed, since that power was based wholly upon the accuracy, the scientific character of the theory?

On the one hand, it could act *as if*. While reality drifts far away from "socialism" as best it can, public utterances and writing describe that reality as "socialism under construction." A schism occurs between reality and pseudo reality. The art of speech consists of a verbal reality that outwardly resembles reality, adheres to it, keeps as close to it as possible. However, the miracle of the *adaequatio rei et intellectus* (the equation of the thing and the intellect)—or, rather, the equation of the thing and the word— never occurs. But the existence of this schism must be denied. Men must therefore contradict reality and confirm pseudo reality by votes, applause, and broad smiles. And that requires terror. "The sole reality," wrote Souvarine, "is terror, which decomposes the mind and poisons the consciousness. The lie is the first corollary of terror." I think that this sentence should be changed to read: "The sole reality is the falsified word, which decomposes the mind and poisons the consciousness." Terror is the first corollary of the lie. Not terror but the lie was first attacked by Solzhenitsyn.

On the other hand, communist power could once again attempt, and keep on attempting, whenever possible, the impossible incarnation. This is the meaning of the two alternative political models described: War Communism, which tries to transform or destroy all resistance to the Party's actions, and the NEP, which tries to strengthen the Party—that is, to perfect and consolidate the mold into which reality once again will be poured.

These two steps could demand of the Party considerable skill, tactical sense, and political depth. But they are fundamentally simple. In short, they are inaugural, initial, preliminary steps, even though they have not met with success in sixty years of trying. Blood work has been done, but the first stone of the edifice of socialism has not yet been laid. This is why such a crude scheme as War Communism and the NEP controls and gives meaning to so many events and facts. In succession, one party line or the other must always be taken up again and begun anew. Because the two lines each fail in turn, and because there are no others, the scheme repeats itself inexorably.

Have I come close to an answer? Why, I repeat, isn't it as clear as day, and why aren't the Soviets taken seriously when they explain all this in their handbooks? Is it really necessary, in order to understand such a simple, openly stated system, to have deep first-hand knowledge of Soviet reality (to have lived in the country, to have been a communist), or to have metaphysically experienced nothingness? I do not exclude this completely, but there are more everyday reasons for our lack of understanding. Let us return to international society and its foreign policy toward the U.S.S.R. Let us discuss rapidly two very effective but equally incomprehensible causes: lack of information and the false symmetry.

Lack of information: the U.S.S.R. cloaks itself in secrecy. Making the most of détente, it effectively controls sources of information about itself: foreign correspondents in Moscow, newspaper editors in European capitals, the radio, and television. In the name of détente, a common aim of both East and West, it is easy to hint that the media should be discreet. Next—must we admit it?—come fear and cowardice. They are excusable. God only knows what can happen. But the blunder of those who sincerely want to know is intellectually most interesting.

These people, moreover, vaguely suspect their blunder.

The preponderant influence that Russia has won through surprise . . . frightened the people of the West, who accepted it fatalistically, and only resisted by fits and starts. But in addition to fascination, skepticism is continually being reborn and follows fascination like a shadow, mingling the light note of irony with the cries of dying peoples, mocking the true greatness of Russian strength as a posture assumed by a buffoon to dazzle and deceive. Other empires in their infancy have caused similar doubts to arise; but Russia has become a colossus without having dissipated them.

These words of Karl Marx are more applicable to Soviet Russia than to the Russia of Nicholas I.

I propose the following hypothesis: our difficulty in understanding the Soviet world stems in large part from our natural and deliberate tendency to establish a symmetry between that world and our own. The human mind was made to live in a homogeneous world. Communication with someone else implies that we both share the same reality. In its desire to have the U.S.S.R. join the community of nations, international society—like the communist movement itself—has been led to act *as if*. When negotiating with the Soviet State, which takes pains to deny that reality has been split in two, international society has, on the occasion of each treaty, each statement of principles, been willingly or unwillingly led to do the same. To this absolutely new historical formulation, Sovietologists themselves are forced, by their habitual turn of mind, to apply categories that they consider universal, but that are nonetheless exceptions in this instance.

I have pointed out the ambiguity of the concept of *economy* when applied to the Soviet system of production. The notion of Soviet *society* is itself debatable, if one conceives of society as a body of individuals among whom there are organized relationships and reciprocal services, consolidated into institutions. The institutions are fictitious or decorative, and there is no reciprocity between civil society and the Party-State, which, since it lives upon ideology, cannot see civil society for what it is. Can we even speak of a Soviet *regime* without recalling that it fits into neither Aristotle's nor Montesquieu's categories, that it does not correspond to the known forms of good government—although it claims to be a synthesis of them all— or the known forms of bad government? I repeat: it is neither a tyranny nor a true despotism.

But if the fundamental notions and basic concepts become inadequate and require recasting when applied to the Soviet world, what will happen to the fragile edifices built upon those foundations? Some individuals, carried away by their desire to see similarities, have pondered over the

"convergence" between East and West, have even dis-
coursed about the Soviet "military-industrial complex."
The craze for symmetry is responsible for the shallow
but widespread image of the "two empires," Soviet and
American. This image sees as similar—this time with
condemnation—repression in Chile and in the U.S.S.R.,
a Mediterranean dictator and the dictator in the Kremlin.
But there is no dictator in the Kremlin. The West's diplomacy of détente takes into account the necessary coexistence
of different economies and societies, different regimes, and
in the process grants the Soviet government official recognition of what it is vainly trying to achieve: an economy, a
society, a regime. The mightiest power on earth obliges its
subjects to espouse this recognition, which it obtains from
international society by the simple mechanism of negotiation.

This leads to several drawbacks for the partners of the
U.S.S.R. Following the logic of symmetry, they concentrate
upon the system of inter-state activity (System B) in Soviet
foreign policy, and lose sight of its relationship to the
system of ideological activity (System A). The latter seems
to them a survival from the past, a superficial formality.
It dims their political vision. Another drawback in negotiating on the level of pseudo reality is that reality is abandoned
to its unhappy fate. The Russian, Ukrainian, Georgian,
Armenian, and other peoples have endured all they have
endured without asking for sympathy, or the simple expression of pity that under other circumstances helped
Ireland, Greece, and Poland to hold fast. These peoples
will not forget this abandonment. In the religious domain
it will be costly. The blood of these martyrs, who do not
appear on any church calendar, cries out. Through spiritual
sloth, all too many churchmen in the West compare the

communist world to the barbarian world, and fancy they will convert that communist world, just as they baptized Clovis and Vladimir. But the barbarians had fine weapons, handsome stirrups, imposing stature: they existed. Where is "socialism"? Can we hope to give an extra dose of soul to something that has no body? To put it in theological terms, these same individuals picture the communist world as a state of nature, and a well-oriented one at that, which lacks only grace. Alas, it is not grace that is lacking, but nature.

This formal recognition of pseudo reality by international society, which thus gives it reality, tempts me to christen it a "moral" Witte system. Like its economic analogue, it involves international society and carries it along. Can international society morally oppose this socialism that it has acknowledged as existing, and therefore as better? How could it prefer instead what it gradually is being forced to call capitalism?

And yet one must negotiate. But how?

I shall quote Michelet again: "Since Russia, its nature, its own life, is a lie, its foreign policy and its military arm against Europe are necessarily a lie."

Well, here we must be wary of overly obvious comparisons. Michelet, Marx, and even Custine* are all the more misleading about Soviet Russia because they seem to be so very true. Indeed, they reinforce the illusion of a continuity between the old Russian regime and the Soviet regime. Yet that is precisely where the sharpest break occurred. The Soviet lie is incomparably more heady than the traditional Russian lie, because it is not a lie. It is a false pretense of a lie, a lying lie, a pseudo lie. In that country everything is false, even the lie.

* The Marquis de Custine (1790–1857), author of *La Russie en 1839*.

A lie is an assertion that is knowingly contrary to the truth, that is made with the intention of deceiving. It was an art at which the Empire of the tsars was a past master. When Catherine II declared that the Russian peasant was basically freer than the German and French peasants, she was lying. But she knew the truth. The Russian governments of the Old Regime employed—perhaps more successfully than others—the classical Machiavellian lie, with which you deceive your partner about reality in order to accomplish your goals. But the tsar's ministers had the same idea as their partners about what reality was. They had two words, designating one and the same reality, and they held these words in common with those partners. The latter were not obliged to be truthful either, but they knew what the truth was. When, on the pretext of protecting the Holy Land, the Russian army advanced upon Constantinople, each side knew that Constantinople was the real goal; using a similar pretext, Britain then set about barring Russia's path. Two words, one reality. But when Brezhnev, after Lenin, declares that the Soviet citizen is the freest in the world, he is not lying. He is basing his statement upon pseudo reality, where words receive a new and very specific meaning. According to that same ideological reality, the Swiss citizen does not enjoy freedom.

The opposite of the lie is truth, which is given a different name. Within ordinary reality, the opposite of freedom is slavery. If two people in a conversation agree upon the same word, but not upon the reality to which it refers, that same word will mean two different things. And so the opposite of freedom, in the Soviet sense, is what we call freedom. The opposite of détente is détente. The opposite of the defense of peace is the defense of peace. Contrary to the accepted idea, the Soviet world is characterized not by double-talk but by single-talk—single-talk within duplicate realities. One word, two realities.

The perfect communist is one who, in imitation of Lenin, has only one word, only one language, and who lives entirely within pseudo reality. If he lies—except to the class enemy, to whom it is his duty to lie—he is not a good communist. If he believes that the language he uses can have recourse to "real" reality, he is naive. If in his inner heart, or in the company of his friends, he speaks another language, he is a cynic. A good communist is perfectly sincere.

A negotiation generally is carried out on two levels, the concrete level and the level of principles. For obvious reasons, on the concrete level one must negotiate indefatigably with the Soviet government. One must patiently seek agreements—temporary, like all agreements between sovereign states—about frontiers, trade, armaments, exchanges. In these negotiations the parties discuss the same things. They have at their disposal the entire arsenal of lies, tricks, Machiavellianism, in order to attain their goals, and that way things work well.

It is on the level of principles that the negotiation risks going awry. The negotiation gradually slides in the direction of principles, owing to the difficulties it encounters on concrete matters. When no agreement can be reached on rockets, it is tempting to declare that both sides are sincerely devoted to peace. When there is disagreement over Vietnam, Angola, Portugal, why not state that in principle both sides are equally attached to nonintervention and the peoples' right to self-determination. But stating a principle poisons the negotiations and makes the Western partner contradict himself. For it is the Americans who are making the rockets, who are intervening in Vietnam, while the

U.S.S.R. is defending peace and fighting imperialism. In this way pseudo reality invades and disorients reality.

Here, then, is the rule that I think should govern negotiations: deal with reality and do not deal with pseudo reality. This is a strict rule. It is so much easier to "carry on a dialogue"—that is, to question the Soviets about their intentions (they want peace, justice, freedom)—than it is to achieve a precarious, patched-up settlement, a settlement that will be called in question again someday, a settlement without glory or moral reward.

Holding discussions with the Soviet government when it is lying, but refusing to discuss when it is sincere, requires unremitting asceticism and effort on our part. In the face of this strange Manichaeanism that summons forth another reality, however, there is no other way than to hold fast to the *one* reality. Confronted by a hallucination, a mirage, a phantasmagoria, we have no other recourse than to practice using our judgment. This is the principle. Therein lies our strength. It is up to the authorities to decide just how it should be used.